The Guilty Soul's
Guide to
Grace

The Guilty Soul's
Guide to
Grace

Sam Laing

DPI
DISCIPLESHIP
PUBLICATIONS
INTERNATIONAL

The Guilty Soul's Guide to Grace
© 2005 by Discipleship Publications International
5016 Spedale Court, #331
Spring Hill, Tennessee 37174

All Scripture quotations, unless indicated, are taken from
the NEW INTERNATIONAL VERSION.
Copyright ©1973, 1978, 1984 by the International Bible Society.
Used by permission of Zondervan Publishing House.
All rights reserved.

The "NIV" and "New International Version" trademarks
are registered in the United States Patent Trademark Office
by the International Bible Society.
Use of either trademark requires the permission of
the International Bible Society.

Printed in the United States of America

ISBN: 1-57782-196-3

Cover Design: Brian Branch
Interior Design: Thais Gloor

To Tom and Sheila Jones,

For showing us all how to live
graciously and courageously

Contents

Introduction 9

UNDERSTANDING GRACE
  1 Free Grace 15
  2 Rich, Lavish Grace 18
  3 The Unsearchable Riches of Grace 20
  4 You Are God's Delight.................................23
  5 Jesus Did Not Change God's Mind About You 26
  6 God Is Not Like Whoever It Was
     Who Rejected You.....................................28
  7 Grace Personified......................................30
  8 Face the Facts of Grace 33
  9 What the Law Does for You 35
 10 The Romance of Grace...............................39
 11 Grace and Wrath 42
 12 We Need Grace to Understand Grace 47

ACCEPTING GRACE
 13 Trusting in Grace......................................51
 14 Feeling 'In Grace' 55
 15 Grace and Commitment 61
 16 Grace and Repentance 68
 17 Grace and Baptism....................................72
 18 Gifted by Grace 77
 19 Godly Sorrow, Worldly Sorrow 85
 20 What Advantage to Always Feeling Guilty? 91
 21 Grace and Self-Rejection 95

22 Desperate for Grace...98
23 Claiming Grace 108

LIVING IN GRACE

24 Grace and Discipline...115
25 When the Guilty Soul Really Is Guilty 120
26 Grace and Adversity 128
27 Grace in the Hour of Need....................................135
28 Grace and Pride 138
29 Grace and Worry 141
30 Grace and Regret..145
31 Grace and Fear...153
32 Grace and Security..159
33 Grace and Human Approval 164
34 Grace and Criticism..169
35 The Grace to Forgive 176
36 Free at Last!...181

Introduction

I would love to say I have a grasp of grace that equals my grasp of being a "Guilty Soul," but I would be lying if I did. Grace is difficult for me to grasp and accept in my mind, but especially difficult for me to accept in my heart. And that, of course, causes me to feel guilty. I read of the rapturous reveries of some souls as they contemplate the glorious grace of God and feel that I live in another universe. I wonder what it is that blocks me from a deeper understanding of this most wonderful and vital spiritual reality.

I have been a Guilty Soul as long as I can remember. I was the kind of kid who always thought that the teacher's rebuke of the whole class was really meant specifically for me. Always a bit uneasy, never entirely comfortable and at peace, I felt a bit out of place in the world. If I got a good grade, I wondered if the teacher missed a mistake somewhere. Oh, I was good, but never good enough. Somehow I sensed that even though others had more egregious sins, sins of the "neon" variety, that my sins of the more muted hues, were deeply, ineluctably true, and perhaps more heinous.

I would love to say that after my conversion to Christ, I entered into a new phase of life, that I shook off the dark and brooding clouds of introspection and self-condemnation, but that is not the truth. Oh yes, I felt and knew the joy of forgiveness, my life deeply changed, and I found a purpose and a source of love that has never failed me...ever. But my tendency to feel guilty, to look at the worst side of myself, to feel under some sort of vague displeasure, has been something that has been slow to change, even with the study of the Scriptures and countless prayers to make the message of glorious grace take its rightful place in my heart and mind. I want to blissfully accept it, but something unknowable and unfathomable within me rises, oozes up from my DNA, my bone marrow, to militate against this understanding.

I do not wish to say that I have not grown, because I have. I do not wish to say that I have not learned, for I have. I do not wish to say that I do not believe more in the loving kindness of my heavenly Father than I ever have, because I do. I am just trying to say that there is something inside me that resists accepting grace.

Perhaps I don't trust myself to accept it with the headlong abandon that I should because I fear I would lessen my devotion or become complacent. Perhaps I suffer from plain old unbelief: it's just too good to be true, all this grace stuff. Maybe deep down inside, I am still prideful and desirous of proving myself, and to hear myself say that makes me feel rather guilty, to be perfectly frank.

So, this is a book written by a guy who has to work very hard to accept grace. I have trouble eradicating the "works" theology from accepting grace, you see! This is not a book by someone who lives deliriously, happily, dreamily in a state of grace. This is a book by the guiltiest of Guilty Souls, a man whose instinct has been, and is, to feel guilty and out of sorts with God.

I do walk closely with God, mind you. I spend most every morning in deep and honest study of his word, and in heartfelt, to-the-bone honest prayer. I love God, this I know. And I know he loves me. I love Jesus, too, and I know he loves me.

I have the Holy Spirit, and I have seen him do his mighty works time and time again in my life—sometimes in a moment and sometimes over the years, as if growing a great oak tree.

Yet, I feel the guilt. I feel the pain of my deep selfishness, *— I feel the same way* of my unbelief, of my tendencies to laziness, pride, bitterness and fear. All of these things grieve me deeply, and I know that God sees them more plainly than I. I know Jesus died for my sins, and I believe his blood alone is sufficient to save me. I am convinced that no amount of tears, repentance, good works or striving for sincerity or humility will ever earn my forgiveness. I know that only the grace of God can do that.

I realize that some of my readers will not readily identify with these issues. You might even wonder how people could get themselves into such a state. In this book when I refer to a Guilty Soul, I am referring especially to those who battle with themselves and their consciences is this way. But the truth is, all of us are Guilty Souls even if we do not greatly struggle with guilt feelings. We have all sinned, we are all guilty before God, and we all desperately need grace. Without it we are all lost. Every person who is saved is a guilty person, saved by grace through faith. It is just that Guilty Souls feel more condemned and have more battles with their conscience than others. But the others of you need to come along and expand your grasp of grace and also learn many ways it is to be applied to our lives.

I will walk with you through these pages in search of grace. I do believe that grace is indeed amazing, the greatest gift God has given, purchased with his Son's precious blood. I believe that when Christians learn to grasp grace, we can experience a freedom and joy that no one else on earth can possess. We will talk about it on the most down-to-earth level we can. As we search for grace, I believe we will come to realize the glorious truth that grace is even more earnestly looking for us. May we together find it and be found by it, accept it, grasp it, live in it, rejoice in it, and be transformed by it.

—Sam Laing
Athens, Georgia

Editor's note: In most of the books we publish, we require the chapters to be somewhat consistent in word count. With *The Guilty Soul's Guide to Grace*, we began to edit with this policy in mind. However, we made the decision to leave the chapter lengths as they are because this seems to express the nature of the book best. This is a presentation of thoughts about grace, and quite simply, in life some thoughts are longer than others.

So, enjoy this unconventional approach as the author shares his short and long thoughts about grace with you.

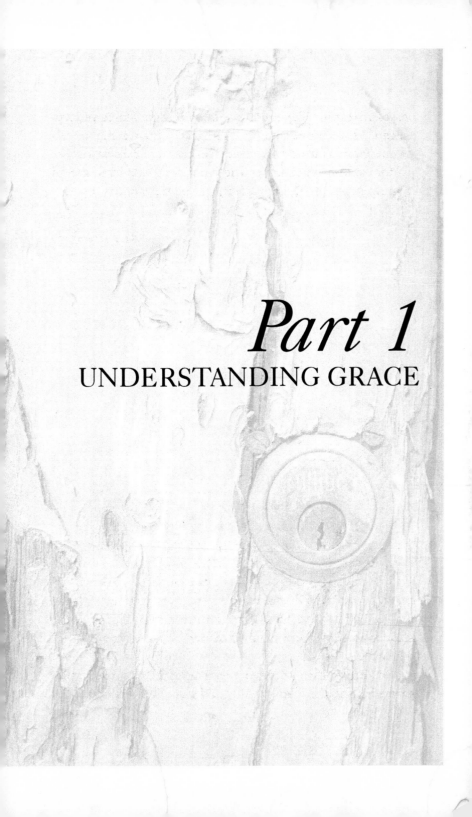

Part 1
UNDERSTANDING GRACE

Chapter 1

Free Grace

...for all have sinned and fall short of the glory of God, and are justified freely by his grace through the redemption that came by Christ Jesus.

Romans 3:23–24

Free. That's the only way grace comes. You can't pay for it. You can't earn it. You can't be worthy of it. You will never deserve it. No matter how great your commitment, how costly your sacrifices, how painful your sufferings, you cannot buy your way into a relationship with God. No matter how contrite you are for your sins, no matter how intense your sorrow that you hurt God, you cannot merit a relationship with him. Despite how great your faith, how unbounded your belief in God's care, that trust is only an admission that you are depending on God to do for you what you can never do for yourself.

Regardless of how pure your motives, how sincere your heart, how unselfish your aspirations, you cannot pay the price of the debt that you owe. No matter how hard or how long you work, pray and serve, it is only a gift from God that can save you. When Paul writes, "For it is by grace you have been saved, through faith—and this is not from yourselves, it is the gift of God" (Ephesians 2:8), he means exactly what he says. Salvation is a gift. It was originated and authored by

God, and was purchased by Jesus on the cross. Our deeds can never pay for it, and our faith can only reach out with empty hands to receive it.

Sin was and is our problem. It separates and distances us from a righteous and holy God. We all sin. We sin by what we do and by what we fail to do. Sin is our greatest problem—always has been, always will be. How can God, who loves us, but who can have no fellowship with sin, have a relationship with us? Does he compromise his holiness and take us in as we are? Or, does he forget about us, and let us be forever estranged in our sin?

God has a solution. If sin is regarded as a debt (and it is), then he himself will pay that debt. He will pay the debt at the very highest cost to himself. He will send his Son to pay the debt. He will give up his only Son, the one he loves the most, and the one with whom he has unbroken fellowship and communion. His Son's righteousness is alone sufficient to efface the stain of sin, to pay its immense, incalculable debt.

It will break the heart of the Father to do this. No greater suffering is there than that of a parent for a suffering child.

It will break the heart of Jesus to do this. He will surrender the dignity and honor he has known in heaven. He will know ridicule, suspicion, criticism, humiliation, loneliness, betrayal, misunderstanding and rejection. He will suffer pain beyond description. He will have no one to comfort him, no one on this earth who truly understands. But he will, out of love for his Father and for us, pay that price.

In the end, it will mean joy for us. It will mean we can know God's love and one day share that love and fellowship together in heaven.

All of this is by grace. It is the free gift of God, in which we who are guilty are declared guiltless, as if we had never sinned at all.

And we are not only saved initially by grace, we are sustained by it every moment, every day. The same principle that saved us, keeps us saved. But it is more than a principle that does all this. It is the heart behind the principle; it is the thought and the love of the Father in heaven. It is his soul of giving and caring that saves us. It is the Author of grace who saves us, and saves us freely.

Grace. It is free.

Chapter 2

Rich, Lavish Grace

In him we have redemption through his blood, the forgiveness of sins, in accordance with the riches of God's grace that he lavished on us with all wisdom and understanding.

Ephesians 1:7–8

Grace is more than free; it is richly and lavishly bestowed. Grace is this way because God is a lavish and generous God. He gives, and he gives again; then he gives more. God has unlimited wealth with which to be generous, and he has a heart of love and kindness that calls him to give his wealth away.

David says, "My cup overflows" (Psalm 23:5). Jesus echoes the same sentiments: "I came that they might have life, and might have it abundantly" (John 10:10 NAS). God is not chintzy. He is openhanded and openhearted in his giving. When Jesus fed the 5,000, twelve baskets were left over. When he fed the 4,000, seven baskets were left over.

In describing the generosity of God, Jesus says,

"Give, and it will be given to you. A good measure, pressed down, shaken together and running over, will be poured into your lap. For with the measure you use, it will be measured to you." (Luke 6:38)

When the prodigal son came home after deserting his father and wasting all he had given him, the father did not wait for him to trudge all the way up to him. He ran out, embraced his son, interrupted his apology and poured out upon his son not only his forgiveness, but the privileges of an honored prince. Peter says that one day we will have "a rich welcome" into our eternal home (2 Peter 1:11). We will not just barely make it, but we will be warmly, joyfully received. Such is the abundant generosity of our heavenly Father.

Generosity and lavishness are deep in God's nature. They are essential to who he is. They find their origins in the unplumbed depths of care, compassion and mercy that well up from inside his heart of love.

Every day God gives generously, even to those who do not believe in him, even to those who curse his name. He throws away magnificent sunsets on unseeing, uncaring eyes. He gives the capacity to love to those who choose to love other things and other people in his place, or who fill their hearts with bitterness, hatred and apathy. He sends the song of birds and the cool breezes of springtime to those who do not know him, and who either don't see the beauty of his gifts or feel as if they somehow deserve them.

God is generous, lavish and abundant in his ways, in his heart and in his giving. He is generous in his grace. He wants us to know him. He wants us to know his great love. He wants to share with us the life he has designed for us, and he wants us to live with him now and forever.

Lavish, generous, abundant. More than you need, more than enough to take care of you and every problem and challenge you will ever face. God's grace: it is offered to you, it is waiting for you, as is he.

Chapter 3

The Unsearchable Riches of Grace

Although I am less than the least of all God's people, this grace was given me: to preach to the Gentiles the unsearchable riches of Christ.

Ephesians 3:8

And I pray that you, being rooted and established in love, may have power, together with all the saints, to grasp how wide and long and high and deep is the love of Christ, and to know this love that surpasses knowledge—that you may be filled to the measure of all the fullness of God.

Ephesians 3:17–19

Paul has finally run out of vocabulary. He has no words left to describe his subject in all of its grandeur and greatness. He has to surrender and say, "It is unsearchable; it surpasses our ability to take it all in." That's how it is with grace. It is so good, so wonderful, so magnificent that human verbiage fails it. However great you think grace is, it is far greater. However wonderful you imagine the love of God through Christ to be, it puts your imagination to shame. Not that we Guilty Souls need any more shame. It's just that grace is that good, that great.

Trying to understand grace is like a young child trying to grasp the depths of his parents' love. It just can't happen. A child simply does not yet have the capacity to do that. In time, understanding will grow. And with it will come the feelings that warm the heart and give light to the life of that child. Perhaps one day the child will grow and have children of his own. Then, he will understand more, and as enlightenment dawns, his heart will say, "Oh, this is how my parents felt about me all those years, and I have never understood until now."

But the love of human parents pales beside our Father's love. This love is so great that Paul prays for us to be given supernatural enlightenment to grasp it. Thanks Paul, we need it! We need the help of God's Holy Spirit; we need the dawning of light from on high to help us understand the greatness of our Father's love and grace.

How well do you understand it? How much better is your understanding today than yesterday, now than before? However much we understand, we have so very far to go. We have so much to see, so much to learn. Our understanding is so limited. We are contained in our little world, boxed up in our little domain. We are like a child who can only see the confines of his crib or of his tiny room. Outside of our world, beyond our limited environment, there is a great universe waiting to be seen, to be explored and enjoyed. More than that, there is a God who made that universe, and who wants us to know him and his love.

God longs for us to progress in our knowledge. He knows that growth in understanding leads to growth of capacities. Let us be eager to grow in our understanding. Let us expand our minds. Let us enlarge our hearts. Let us allow our imaginations to have free play, to run wild. However much we imagine, there is infinitely more to discover. Go ahead. Try to outdo God's love and grace in the uncharted realms of your thought world. You will fall short. No matter how big you think God and his love are, how vast the love of his Son, it is far, far greater and far more wonderful than your wildest dreams.

Chapter 4

You Are God's Delight

For the LORD takes delight in his people;
he crowns the humble with salvation.
Psalm 149:4

"I think God likes me a lot. I've always thought that." So said my wife at a family communion service. My daughter Alexandra, my son Jonathan and I looked at each other and broke out laughing. We are all Guilty Souls, you see, and it just struck us as funny.

Guilty Souls have to have something to laugh about, I suppose.

The topic that morning was taken from the title of the next chapter in this book, "Jesus Did Not Change God's Mind About You." We all looked up verses that talked about how much God loves us. Geri pointed out from Isaiah 43:4 that we are precious and honored in God's sight. I shared about God delighting in us (Psalm 147:11). We talked about how most parents delight in their children and despite knowing the very worst traits in their kids, love and treasure them anyway.

Later on in our devotional I asked, "What has Mom's belief in God liking her and delighting in her, done for her?

Has it hurt her or helped her? Has it made her a better or worse person?"

The unanimous answer was that her belief had done nothing but make her a delightful person. Geri is one of the happiest, most caring, loving and unselfish people I have ever known. Our kids heartily agree. She is sparkling and joyful, a true delight to be around. Far from making her a self-centered, self-absorbed, egotistical soul, her belief that "God likes me a lot" has made her more loving and lovable.

Let's face it: isn't one of the reasons we reject God's approval because we are afraid if we let ourselves off the hook, we will become self-absorbed, unspiritual and arrogant? It's that way for me, and I rather suspect it is the same for many other Guilty Souls out there. We think if we don't properly berate and beat ourselves into submission, we will end up abandoning God and becoming spoiled, selfish egotists. We think our pride is such a lurking beast within us that to give ourselves any sort of affirmation would let it out of its cage, and expose us for the spiritual werewolves we really are.

God does not have such a low estimate of us. He believes that the best way to make us loving is to love us first. He believes that if he loves us in a personal, affectionate way, that it will bring out the best, not the worst, in us. He believes that if he likes us and smiles at us, we will smile back at him and at others as well.

Do you believe God could smile at you? Can you even imagine such a thing? I think he does. He even did so in the Old Testament, back when many of us think he was all mad with everybody.

> "The LORD bless you
>   and keep you;
> the LORD make his face shine upon you

and be gracious to you;
the LORD turn his face toward you
and give you peace." (Numbers 6:24–26)

Do you believe God could regard you as a treasure, as precious? See his heart for his people:

For you are a people holy to the LORD your God. The LORD your God has chosen you out of all the peoples on the face of the earth to be his people, his treasured possession. (Deuteronomy 7:6)

Since you are precious and honored in my sight,
    and because I love you,
I will give men in exchange for you,
    and people in exchange for your life.
(Isaiah 43:4)

Don't you think it is time you started agreeing with God? Why don't you let him love and like you for a change? See what happens. If afterwards you grow fangs, a wooly coat and start baying at the moon, we'll just have to find a wooden stake or a silver bullet and put you out of your misery. But I don't think it will happen. I think you will start enjoying your life a lot more. I think you will start smiling more and having more fun being a Christian. I think you will start treating other people better. I'll bet you will become more dedicated, more zealous, more eager to tell others about Jesus. And, most important: my guess is that you will stay faithful until the end of your life.

Chapter 5

Jesus Did Not Change God's Mind About You

> This is how God showed his love among us: He sent his one and only Son into the world that we might live through him.
>
> 1 John 4:9

Jesus did not come into the world and change the way God felt about you. He came and showed you how God felt about you all along. Some of us have the idea that God never really liked us a lot anyway and that Jesus had to talk him into it. We imagine that Jesus, being the good and loving guy that he was, after coming down here and finding out how hard it was to be a human being, was able to go back to heaven and talk God into feeling better about us.

Is that the way you look at it? Rather, is that the way you look at God? He's the Perfect One, but he has a bad attitude. He sees right through us, sees us as we are, and he doesn't really like us, so Jesus talks him out of it. Jesus is on our side, but God is not. God condemns us, resents us, doesn't like us, but Jesus convinces him otherwise.

That's not the way it is. The Bible says,

> "For *God so loved the world that he gave his one and only Son*, that whoever believes in him shall not perish but have eternal life." (John 3:16, emphasis mine)

God *so loved!* That tells us something profoundly important about God. It tells us Jesus is the *proof* of his love, not the *cause* of his love. God loved us before Jesus came and died for us. God loved us before our sin was taken away by the blood of Jesus. God loved us before Jesus came to earth. God loved us tenderly and dearly, and longed for a relationship with us before Jesus died to make that relationship possible.

God is love (1 John 4:16). He is all about love. He made us *because* he loved and he made us *to* love. Jesus is the ultimate way his love was, and is, expressed. And Jesus is the way that God's love is to be enjoyed.

Jesus enables us to be close to God, to be forgiven by God, to be reconciled to God. He does not enable God to love us, but he enables God to be near to us. And that is a very good thing to know.

Chapter 6

God Is Not Like Whoever It Was Who Rejected You

Though my father and mother forsake me,
   the LORD will receive me.

Psalm 27:10

If an enemy were insulting me,
   I could endure it;
if a foe were raising himself against me,
   I could hide from him.
But it is you, a man like myself,
   my companion, my close friend,
with whom I once enjoyed sweet fellowship
   as we walked with the throng at the house of God.

Psalm 55:12-14

Most of us who struggle to accept grace have God confused with somebody else. Somebody we could not please. Somebody we could not win over. Somebody who gave us no attention or who gave up on us. God is not like whoever it was who rejected you, and they might not have really rejected you anyway.

So, who was it for you?

For me, it was my dad. I was the classic "My dad didn't

love me, didn't like me" case. My dad passed away when I was twelve. It took me a few months of thinking it through after I was forty years old to come to understand that my view of my dad was very wrong. But it was my view, and without consciously adopting it, I believed it within my deepest self. That was not my dad's fault. It was just the way I took things. I would have done it with someone else if not him. It's just the way my mind worked. And because I deeply embedded these thoughts in my mind and emotions, I easily transferred them to God.

God is not like my dad or yours. He is infinitely more loving, more caring, more understanding than any earthly father.

If you are confusing God with someone who rejected you, kick those thoughts out of your head. Stop worshiping your old idol. It is ironic that we create idols that demand of us and do not give back. They demand our worship, our sacrifice, our obeisance, and yet offer no intimacy, no deep acceptance, no profound love. You need to go on an idol-smashing binge worthy of an Old Testament prophet. Cast down that idol that leers at you, that hates you, that can barely stand the sight of you, whom you can never please. Tear down the idol that is ever angry with you, ever displeased, ever fault-finding, and replace it with the Living God, the God of the Bible.

We are the ones in the rejecting business. It is we who reject God and who reject one another.

God is not like us. God is always eager to forgive and to have a relationship with us. He lets us make our own decision, and he will not and cannot have a relationship with us unless we deal with our sin. But he is still not like whoever it was who rejected you, and they may not have really rejected you anyway.

Chapter 7

Grace Personified

The Word became flesh and made his dwelling among us. We have seen his glory, the glory of the One and Only, who came from the Father, full of grace and truth.... From the fullness of his grace we have all received one blessing after another. For the law was given through Moses; grace and truth came through Jesus Christ.

John 1:14, 16–17

Grace is more than a concept. It is more than a theory. It is a person. The reason there is a concept, a theology, is that someone created it. More than creating it, that concept represents all that the person is, all that he thinks and feels.

That person is God, of course. And God expresses his grace through a person, and that person reflects him absolutely in his ways, thoughts and purposes (John 14:9–10).

So, if you have a hard time with the concept, look to where it originated. Look to *whom* it came from. It came from God and was expressed and embodied in Jesus.

Was not Jesus gracious? Was he not, in the flesh, up close and personal, the great illustration of grace? He was grace walking, talking, breathing. He was grace in action.

His message was full of grace. He told parables like the "Prodigal Son and Elder Brother" to show the tender, plead-

30

ing grace of God the Father. He said over and over again, "Go in peace; your sins are forgiven." He had a message of good news to tell. News that swept through a land and people long thirsting and starving for the refreshment of a God who loved them and for the mercy of a Father who could forgive. He proclaimed a manner of serving that was based on love and filial affection rather than the keeping of laws set forth by a distant and impersonal judge.

His example was full of grace. He showed kindness and patience with his most intimate followers, who so misunderstood him and his message, and who remained petty, self-centered and self-serving even after knowing him for so long. So self-consumed were they that on the eve of his arrest, as he was telling them of his coming sacrifice for their sins, they quarreled over who was the greatest. He showed no disgust, no disappointment; he poured the cup, broke the bread, and got down on his hands and knees and washed their feet.

When they failed him, Jesus took them back. He restored Peter to service after his craven and prideful denial. He did more than that: he gave him a place of service, of trust—even of honor—in allowing him to be the first to proclaim the message of the resurrection and open the doors of the church to the lost world.

When Jesus was persecuted and blasphemed by Saul, he himself sought him out and gave him a chance to believe, repent and be saved. And he then gave him the great mission of preaching to the ends of the earth that same message that he had so virulently opposed. Is it any wonder that Saul, the man who was the worst of sinners, became Paul, the grateful proclaimer and defender of grace?

Jesus treated everyone with grace. When his critics sought to discredit and embarrass him by bringing to him the woman they had caught in adultery, asking "What do you say?" he bent down, wrote on the ground, raised himself up, and said, "Let whoever is without sin cast the first stone." He then resumed his writing. He could have scolded them. He could have embarrassed them. He could have shown disgust, scorn and anger. He simply asked a question that exposed to them the shame of their own hearts...and let them walk away. (See John 8:1–11.)

He could have shamed the woman. He could have ignored her. He could have pretended there was no offense in her. Grace would not allow it. He did not condemn, and he sent her on her way with the gracious admonition, "Neither do I condemn you. Go now, and leave your life of sin." For perhaps the first time in her life, this woman met a man who looked upon her as someone worthy of respect and affirmation, and who neither excused nor condemned, but who thought her capable of choosing to live a better life.

He was gracious in his manner. Once a young man came up to ask what he had to do to inherit eternal life. A good young man, raised in the faith of his fathers, obedient to its precepts. Jesus looked at him and loved him. Wouldn't it have been wonderful to see the look in those eyes? Wouldn't you love to have them look upon you? He had some challenging words to say, but they were graciously said, with a facial expression that emitted from a heart of pure love. (See Mark 10:17–22.)

So if you struggle to understand the concept of grace, look to the man who embodies it. Look to the One who is the perfect expression of it, the One who was, and is, full of grace and truth. And see him coming to you and treating you just as graciously as he treated those he met when he walked the earth.

Chapter 8

Face the Facts of Grace

Therefore, since we have been justified through faith,
we have peace with God through our Lord Jesus
Christ, through whom we have gained access by faith
into this grace in which we now stand. And we rejoice
in the hope of the glory of God.

Romans 5:1–2

Grace is a fact, not a feeling. It is true whether you feel it
or not. It is a fact based not on emotion or on your mood. It is
based upon the nature of God and the truth of what Jesus did
for you on the cross.

It is a good thing to feel the grace of God. It is a very good
thing to accept it both mentally and emotionally, but sometimes our minds are weak and our emotions are ephemeral.
Grace is a solid rock and a fact of history. It is based on deeds
done, promises made, promises kept...by God. Do not think
that you are more saved when you *feel* you are more saved.
You are just as saved when your mood is out of sorts and distant as when you feel you can almost hear the singing of the
angels of heaven.

Grace is a place you are *in*. It is where you stand. (See 1
Peter 5:12.) It is a spiritual position you occupy, not a mere
state of mind or feeling. You stand in grace because you have

heard what God's word says about grace and accepted it according to those terms. It is a place you are in because God placed you there at a point in time, the point when you entered into union with Christ in baptism (Romans 6:3–4, Colossians 2:12).

Christians are *constantly* in a state of grace. It is one of the wonderful, mysterious blessings we receive at baptism as we are clothed with Christ through faith (Galatians 3:26). We don't stand "in grace" when we're sinless, then jump "out of grace" every time we sin. That's why Jesus came—to allow us to remain in God's presence, in spite of our sins. Let that sink in for a moment. You *stand in grace*—to put it another way, you are *always standing* in grace. Now go ahead and let yourself enjoy it!

If you want to feel more "in grace," then think about the facts of your situation. Look at what God says about it in the Bible. As you keep looking at it, contemplating it, imagining it, believing it, your feelings will change. Your mood will improve. Your actual status before God will not have changed one iota, but you will certainly feel a lot better, and you will be healthier spiritually and emotionally.

Do not confuse the feelings with the facts. The facts were there before the feelings, and are not based on feelings. Get the facts in your head. As Churchill used to say, "Facts are stubborn things." You better believe it. *Just the facts, ma'am.* Tell your mixed-up feelings to take a hike. They will change for the better after about twenty minutes of contemplation of the facts. Try it. Face the facts of grace.

Chapter 9

What the Law Does for You

> We know that the law is spiritual; but I am unspiritual, sold as a slave to sin.
>
> Romans 7:14

What is the role of law in the life of a Christian? Paul discusses our relationship to the law in Romans, chapter 7. In it, he tells us that the law does three things for us.

The Law Defines Sin

> I would not have known what sin was except through the law. (Romans 7:7)

The law has an important, but unpleasant, task to perform: it has to tell us what sin is so that we can know that we are sinners. We are all capable of immense rationalization. We can justify, excuse and lie to ourselves. We need a straight edge to show us how crooked we are. We need the truth about our sins jammed right in our face so we can see it and not walk away unmoved.

This is what the law does. It tells us what is right and wrong. Sometimes we think grace has no need of the law, but this is incorrect thinking. Without the law we would never know our need of grace. We might think that we are so good and righteous on our own that we really don't need God or we don't need his forgiveness. But the law takes care of that. It tells us the truth about our sin. It tells us what our sins are. You can't get to grace without going through the law. As Paul says in Galatians 3:24, the law is a "schoolmaster" that leads us to Christ (KJV).

The Law Arouses Sin

> For sin, seizing the opportunity afforded by the commandment, produced in me every kind of covetous desire. (Romans 7:8)

Paul observes that sin, by using the law as a springboard, actually tempted him even more. Isn't that how it works? We see a prohibition in God's word, and it seems the "forbidden" becomes all the more attractive, and the opportunities to indulge become more numerous than ever. But even here, God has a gracious purpose:

> The law was added so that the trespass might increase. But where sin increased, grace increased all the more, so that, just as sin reigned in death, so also grace might reign through righteousness to bring eternal life through Jesus Christ our Lord. (Romans 5:20–21)[1]

---

[1]Note that in Romans 7:21 Paul uses the word "law" with a different meaning than in the previous verses. In this case he is not referring to the Old Testament Law of Moses (the Torah), but to a principle he discovered in trying to keep the Torah. The principle he discovered was that when he tried to do good, he failed. Sin tempted, seduced, defeated and enslaved him through the weakness of his human nature. Paul notes that even though in his inner self he gave mental assent to God's will, sin still won the battle. This is not what he wanted, but it is where he ended up. Neither Paul nor any of us is strong enough, even with the highest mental resolve, to conquer sin on our own power. This is the "law" Paul, and all of us, in our experience discover. Only by the grace of God and by the gracious gift of the Holy Spirit (see chapter 8 of Romans), can we find, as we grow in Christ, the strength to overcome sin.

The law does arouse sin, but this is the design of God to help us see our need so that we will turn to him to receive his grace.

The Law Condemns Sin

The final and most somber work of the law is to condemn sin. The law pronounces God's righteous judgment upon sin. It tells of the result of sin: separation from God.

> I found that the very commandment that was intended to bring life actually brought death. For sin, seizing the opportunity afforded by the commandment, deceived me, and through the commandment put me to death. So then, the law is holy, and the commandment is holy, righteous and good. (Romans 7:10–12)

So, Guilty Soul, do not look to the law for your salvation. Do not ask it to do what it was never intended to do and what it never can. It defines sin; it arouses sin; it condemns sin, but it can never *deliver from* sin. Only grace can do that. The law is not your enemy, nor is it the culprit. Your enemy is sin. The law is simply a standard that reveals the truth of God. It is good, but it is weak. It is righteous, but it cannot save. It can tell you the truth, but it cannot help you to obey the truth or be free of truth's verdict.

When we ask the law for forgiveness, it will only give judgment. When we ask it for peace, it can only tell us where we have failed. When we ask it to give us strength, it can only say, "Here is the standard" and "You can never do enough."

Grace agrees with the righteous standards of the law, but it brings good news. It says, "The law is true, but here is the way of forgiveness. Here is the way to find strength. Here is the way for you to grow. Here is the way to please your Father in heaven."

Go to the law to see the righteousness of God. Go to the law to see how far short you fall. Go to the law to be humbled before God. Let the law show you your weaknesses and your needs. Go there, but don't stay there. The law is a guide to see the righteousness of God, but grace is the means of receiving righteousness from God. Let the law lead you to the One who followed it perfectly and met its requirements on your behalf.

Chapter 10

The Romance of Grace

Do you not know, brothers—for I am speaking to men who know the law—that the law has authority over a man only as long as he lives? For example, by law a married woman is bound to her husband as long as he is alive, but if her husband dies, she is released from the law of marriage. So then, if she marries another man while her husband is still alive, she is called an adulteress. But if her husband dies, she is released from that law and is not an adulteress, even though she marries another man.

So, my brothers, you also died to the law through the body of Christ, that you might belong to another, to him who was raised from the dead, in order that we might bear fruit to God. For when we were controlled by the sinful nature, the sinful passions aroused by the law were at work in our bodies, so that we bore fruit for death. But now, by dying to what once bound us, we have been released from the law so that we serve in the new way of the Spirit, and not in the old way of the written code.

Romans 7:1–6

Grace changes our lives by changing our motives. And it changes our motives by changing the nature of our relationship with God.

Paul describes our life by saying that we are like a woman

who has been married to two different husbands. Our first husband was the law. This husband was a good man, but he was distant. He was righteous, but not helpful. He had high expectations, but did not inspire or enable us to meet them. This was a marriage of dutiful service, but marked by loneliness, failure and frustration.

Such marriages are not uncommon. They may be endured, but they are not enjoyed. There is no fun, joy, romance or excitement in such a union. They may result in faithfulness, but not in a deep soul satisfaction.

Such is the life of the Guilty Soul. Married to the law, the Guilty Soul seeks to be faithful. The rewards are meager and austere: there is the solemn satisfaction of duty done, but little joy or warmth. There may one day be the compromise of the commitment once heroically or grudgingly kept for an affair, or even a complete desertion. A human being should be strong enough to dutifully remain loyal, but without the fulfillment of rewards, the temptations of adultery become more attractive.

The law is just not that great a husband. He himself is faithful, but he offers insufficient encouragement. He notes the failures, but does not praise the successes. He expects much, but gives little. It is not that he is sinful or selfish; it is simply beyond his capacity. He does not understand what is needed, and he cannot provide it.

Marriage is meant to be more than righteous; it is meant to be romantic. There is the possibility of fire, zeal, excitement, mystery and an exultant and fulfilling joy. Marriage is a commitment, but a commitment made out of love. *If this is what it takes to be near to the one I love, then that is what I will do.* We are not committed to commitment. We do not fall in love with commitment. We fall in love with a person, and then we commit to this person so we might always enjoy his or her company. We are moved by *who*, not by *what*.

We do this because we long for a relationship—a relationship of sharing, of knowing and being known, a relationship that completes and enriches our life.

Our second husband is very different from our first one. Our new husband is righteous, just like our old husband, but he is more than that. He is caring. He is compassionate. He is helpful. He is understanding. He is forgiving. He walks beside us all the way. He loves us and likes us. He loves us more than we can ever love him in return. He nurtures, he sees the best, he initiates. He expects a great deal, but it is because his regard for us is so high. He expects much, but he has first given much. He expects much, and we respond because he has won our heart. We serve in a new way—not to earn love, but because we are already loved.

It is not that it is always easy to be all that we should, or that our selfishness never darkens the bright skies of our marriage. That happens, but because we know in our heart of hearts that we could never find anyone else who could ever love us so, we give ourselves back to him, over and over again.

Our new husband has won, and continues to win, our hearts and our affections. As we grow older, the bond becomes deeper, the affection greater, the motives stronger. We find that our lives become more fruitful, more productive. We still serve, but in a different and better way. What was once our tiresome duty has become, in increasing measure, our heartfelt desire and greatest privilege.

Chapter 11

Grace and Wrath

The wrath of God is being revealed from heaven against all the godlessness and wickedness of men who suppress the truth by their wickedness, since what may be known about God is plain to them, because God has made it plain to them.

Romans 1:18–19

All of us also lived among them at one time, gratifying the cravings of our sinful nature and following its desires and thoughts. Like the rest, we were by nature objects of wrath. But because of his great love for us, God, who is rich in mercy, made us alive with Christ even when we were dead in transgressions—it is by grace you have been saved.

Ephesians 2:3–5

How can we reconcile the wrath of God with the grace of God? How can the God who loves so dearly be at the same time a God of wrath?

It is here that Guilty Souls are thrown into the turmoil of doubt and depression. Just about the time we begin to obtain some confidence that God loves and likes us, we read passages like the ones above, and our confidence and mood plummet. We wonder if God is some sort of split personality. It seems that he is fickle, or changeable, or even worse, that

42

behind his smiling face and kind words may lurk a brooding anger that will erupt if we fail to please him.

We cannot ignore or write off these passages. In an effort to believe in grace, some have done this. To do so is entirely inadequate and leaves us with lingering suspicions or leaves us as people who have abandoned the standards of Biblical truth in order to conform to our theology or our emotional needs.

These passages must be dealt with and must be properly understood. Because of them we can neither reject grace nor create a god in our own image. And, in coming to understand these passages, we will come to a deeper understanding of God, of ourselves and of his grace. To understand them we will have to leave behind emotional reasoning and approach the subject as mature Bible students.

At the outset we must gain some proportion. Consider the author and the content of the books of the two passages quoted above.

The author of both is Paul, the great champion of grace. He is the Biblical writer whom God used more than any other to define and explain this wonderful theme. He is the man who defended grace against its enemies, who said that to live under the law was to live under a curse (Galatians 3:13) and who urged us to stand fast and not give up our freedom in Christ (Galatians 5:1). Is this man now contradicting himself? Is he, in his references to wrath, throwing out grace and mercy? Surely we must give Paul more credit for consistency of thought.

The content of the books from which these passages are taken help us have a proper perspective on their meaning. The book of Romans lays out the essentiality of salvation by grace and shows the inability of man to save himself. Does Romans 1:18 contradict the rest of the book?

The same holds true for Ephesians. As we saw in previous chapters, Paul in this letter rhapsodizes about grace and describes it in the most lavish of terms. Does this reference to the wrath of God contradict the rest of his argument? In the very next verse following the reference to wrath, Paul mentions that God has "great love" and that God is "rich in mercy." Is this a contradiction, or could Paul be emphasizing two contrasting, but harmonious, qualities of God?

The problem lies in our understanding, not in an inherent contradiction. It is our limited perception and human weakness that create our inability to reconcile these two contrasting, but not contradictory, attributes of God.

When we try to understand wrath from the context of human anger, we naturally emerge with confused thoughts. In my case, wrath was associated with my father losing his temper. I thought of it as an outburst motivated by rage, disgust, impatience and loss of self-control. Until I matured and understood that my dad's anger was not as serious as I had thought, and that it did not mean that he was disgusted with me or rejected me, I lived under a cloud of insecurity and fear. It is entirely understandable that I transferred that understanding over to God. As I learned of the God of the Bible, I saw his love, but always struggled to understand his displeasure, judgment and discipline. I had deep insecurity about this and had to work to overcome it.

We must understand that God's wrath is not based on sinful, resentful feelings. God reacts to sin, and he is offended by it. Sometimes we see in the Scriptures God's direct judgment or punishment for sin. In the example of Ananias and

Sapphira (Acts 5) God exercises his sovereign, righteous and (in this case) immediate judgment. He does not hate the people he judges. He hates the sin they have committed. He is not acting out of ill temper or malice, but out of righteous indignation.

In human anger, righteous indignation is a rare thing. That is why the Bible warns us about anger (Ephesians 4:26, James 1:19–20). Even in our best moments, anger can degenerate into selfishness or personal resentment. We often become angry without having all the facts or in reaction to a personal affront. We must remember that God knows all the facts and judges justly. We also must recall that he tolerates much disrespect from humanity as a whole. He is "slow to anger, abounding in love" (Psalm 103:8). God never gets angry from selfish impatience or petulant pride.

God regards sin differently than we do. Imagine for a moment an incident that would deeply offend you. But this incident must have to do with an offense that hurts someone else, perhaps someone close to you. Imagine someone insulting or harming your mother, your father, your child, your sibling or your dearest friend. Imagine someone harming an innocent, helpless victim. What emotions rise up within you? How do you feel? Perhaps this can help us understand how God reacts to sin. He is holy, and all sin is an affront to him. He sees sin and reacts to it strongly because of who he is.

Second, God reacts to sin because of its results. He sees what it did to his Son. He sees what it does to those who are sinned against. He sees what it does to those who commit it. This is why God hates sin, and why he hates all sin. He judges it. Sin cannot exist in his holy presence.

But God hates *only* sin; he loves sinners! He loves us in

spite of our sin. He created us. We are made in his image. He loves us because it is his nature to love and because he made us to live in fellowship with him. So, while hating our sin, God loves us, the sinners. He makes provision for our sin to be forgiven and even works to help us accept that provision.

God is not like us. He is never motivated by sin. He is always motivated by love. But God is also unlike us in that he cannot and will not have fellowship with sin. It is impossible for him to do this. He cannot merely wink away sin or lightly dismiss it.

We must trust God. We must seek to understand, but we also must realize that some things about God will always be difficult for us to grasp. We can trust the God of Grace. We can know that the holiness of God and the sin of man that makes grace necessary, do not in any way negate the truth of this amazing grace and of his love that extends it. And in knowing this, we can have peace and confidence.

Chapter 12

We Need Grace to Understand Grace

I keep asking that the God of our Lord Jesus Christ, the glorious Father, may give you the Spirit of wisdom and revelation, so that you may know him better. I pray also that the eyes of your heart may be enlightened in order that you may know the hope to which he has called you, the riches of his glorious inheritance in the saints.

Ephesians 1:17–18

We need grace to help us understand grace. If that is not what Paul is asking for in the prayer recorded above, then I don't know what else he could mean. Grace is a wonderful, amazing thing. Like most things of God, it is far above us. It is above our mental capacity, above our ability to imagine, to conceive, to take in. We need help to understand it. Now that's an amazing thing: we need grace to understand how great grace is.

I have worked and studied to understand grace for more than thirty years. I understand it far better today than I did earlier in my life, but I know that I still don't totally get it. I am glad that a perfect understanding of grace is not a prerequisite for being saved by it, or I, and all of us, would be in trouble.

Here is what Guilty Souls do: we make even the acceptance of grace a form of works. We make understanding grace something that makes us more worthy in God's eyes. But we will never understand grace as we should. How could we? How can we, with our hearts and minds darkened by sin and unbelief, ever really fathom such a sublime concept in all of its greatness and majesty?

The best thing for us to do is accept grace. Admit we need it and also admit we don't know how much we need it. But, in the meantime, enjoy it.

Acceptance is agreeing with God, not fighting him on the subject of our condition before him. It means we agree with God, and that we pray to him to deepen our understanding as time goes by. Should we study and pray to understand more of the grace of God? Absolutely, yes. Should we adopt a nonchalant attitude and take grace for granted? Absolutely not. I know some Christians who have been cast into bondage by feeling that they do not understand or appreciate grace sufficiently. Is this not simply another device of Satan to keep us from enjoying our walk with God and from enjoying the salvation he has given us?

Let us learn to accept grace with all the capacity that we have, knowing that God will grant us deeper understanding the longer we walk with him. We must never let understanding be another form of earning our salvation, as if the depth of our conviction and perception is a means to earn status before God. Let us open our hearts to God to the extent that we can, and humble ourselves to the extent we are able, knowing that in love, God covers the vast distance of our limited understanding with a generous outpouring of grace.

Part 2
ACCEPTING GRACE

Chapter 13

Trusting in Grace

You grumbled in your tents and said, "The LORD hates us; so he brought us out of Egypt to deliver us into the hands of the Amorites to destroy us."
Deuteronomy 1:27

We have to step out and trust God's grace just like we have to step out and trust God in other areas. When we are confronted with a situation in which we feel weak and powerless, we turn to God to strengthen us. When we are uncertain, we depend on God to give us wisdom. When we are afraid, we ask God for courage. To fail to turn to God in such circumstances means that we doubt God's ability to help us and that we believe he is somehow inadequate.

But there is a deeper issue involved here. Beyond our trust in God's *ability* is our trust in his *willingness*. And here is where Guilty Souls struggle the most. Tell me, is it worse to doubt God's ability or his willingness? Which is more debilitating? Both are a form of doubt. On the one hand we doubt God's power, on the other we doubt his love. Somehow, doubting God's love seems to be a less serious form of doubt; it seems more righteous, more holy, more harmless. But are we not doubting God just the same? Is it not just as serious to doubt God's willingness as to doubt his ability?

Let us go back in time to the children of Israel in their wilderness wanderings. What was it that caused them to turn back, to turn away from God? Moses gives us the answer: "You grumbled in your tents and said, 'The LORD hates us; so he brought us out of Egypt to deliver us into the hands of the Amorites to destroy us...'" (Deuteronomy 1:27). And what was Moses' reply? "'You saw how the LORD your God carried you, as a father carries his son, all the way you went until you reached this place'" (Deuteronomy 1:31). Their view was that God hated them, that he didn't like them and wanted to punish them. God's view was that he loved them, liked them, and affectionately cared for them. He assured them that in all of their trials he had carried them like a father carries his son and that their trials were not a sign of his displeasure.

Tell me, Guilty Soul, what is your view of God?

What is it with us? We are just like our spiritual forebears. We have a hard time trusting in the love of God. When we face trials, when we feel weak, or when we fail, we begin to doubt—not just God's ability, but his attitude. This kind of doubt will defeat us just as surely as when we doubt God's power. As a matter of fact, it will hurt us even more.

Let's think about this from God's point of view for a minute. What if you had a child who forever doubted your love for him, a child who would never trust that you cared for him? Would that not harm your relationship with that child just as much, no, more, than doubt in your ability to care for him? Would not the greatest longing of your heart be for that child to trust your love for him above all else?

So how do we get past this?

I've got it: now that you see this problem for what it is, you should feel very guilty, feel like a failure, and lose even more confidence. This is but another sign of your worthlessness and the hopelessness of your situation. Right! That'll get the job done! No, my fellow Guilty Soul, it will not.

Here is what you need to do. <u>First, see this attitude for what it really is—a failure to trust.</u> <u>Next, repent of that attitude, that is, change your mind.</u> Change your mind and believe the truth about God and his nature. Get rid of your false ideas. Not only are they false, they are destructive. They harm your relationship with God, and they harm you and your peace of mind. <u>You need to fight off these attitudes as you would any other destructive attitude.</u>

Stand up for your freedom in Christ (Galatians 5:1). Paul tells us that if we depend on our own performance, then that is what we will be judged on and we "have fallen away from grace" (Galatians 5:4). <u>Do you really want to be judged by your performance?</u> <u>Then stop trusting in it.</u> <u>Trust in the grace given you by your loving Father in heaven.</u>

Trust what God has said about himself. Throw down your idol of the apathetic God who does not care about you. Cast down the idol of the angry, resentful, hateful God who delights in your failures and can't stand the sight of you, the God who is forever displeased. Study and believe the truths about God as revealed in his word: <u>God loves you</u>, <u>likes you</u>, <u>intends good for you</u>, <u>forgives you and wants to help you to grow and change.</u> And when you have done this, and find that the doubt returns, do it again. And again. <u>Every time you are tempted to doubt God's love for you</u>, <u>cast that doubt out of your heart and mind just as you would any other kind of doubt.</u> It's that simple.

It is a step of faith. Just as you have stepped out at other times when you trusted God to strengthen you in times of need, step out and trust God for his grace. He is waiting for you. He cannot and will not break his word. He will be faithful. He is your Father in heaven. And, as he carried his children in the past, he will also carry you—all the way home.

Chapter 14

Feeling 'In Grace'

Finally, brothers, whatever is true, whatever is noble, whatever is right, whatever is pure, whatever is lovely, whatever is admirable—if anything is excellent or praiseworthy—think about such things. Whatever you have learned or received or heard from me, or seen in me—put it into practice. And the God of peace will be with you.

Philippians 4:8–9

As I write this, I am not feeling especially strong about grace in an emotional sense. My heart is not welling up with joy; my eyes are not filled with tears; my memory is not flooded with gratitude; my pulse is normal. So what does that mean? Does it mean I need to get on my knees right here in this bookstore and pray myself into a better emotional state? Does it mean I need to close up shop until I am keenly attuned emotionally? Does it mean something even more ominous—that I am a fraud, that my heart is dead, that I am bereft of gratitude, devoid of love for God and have no relationship to him?

It doesn't mean these things at all. It just means...my emotions are not at a heightened state at the moment.

One of the real issues with Guilty Souls is our dependence

on our emotions to tell us our spiritual condition. <u>Most Guilty</u> <u>Souls I know are people who feel very deeply and who are</u> <u>supremely aware of their emotions.</u>

Let's get this straight right now: there is nothing wrong with being a deeply emotional person. There are lots of them in the Bible: Moses, Jeremiah, David, Peter, Paul (if you don't think so, look up "tears," and see how many times Paul shed them!) and ultimately Jesus himself.

The problem is not our emotions, but in the way we understand our emotional life.

Aside from physical or drug-induced causes, most emotions flow from our thought processes. This is a foundational Biblical teaching and happens to be the fundamental premise of cognitive therapy, a branch of psychological teaching that has in recent years gained many adherents in the mental health community.[1]

In a nutshell, the theory is this: Emotions are a product of thought. Whatever you are feeling at this very moment is a product, not of reality, but of your perceptions and thoughts about reality.

Example: A huge meteorite is at this moment on its way to strike you dead, but you are unaware. Are you afraid? Anxious? Not at all. You are about to be incinerated, and you are blissfully placid. Are your perceptions based in reality? No. You are ignorant. Your emotions, in this case, are betraying you.

Another example: There is no meteorite on the way to strike you, but you think there is. You are nervous, frightened, out of your mind with fear. Are your fears accurate? No. Do

---

[1]An excellent book on the subject is *Feeling Good: The New Mood Therapy* by David D. Burns, MD., mass market edition published by Avon Books, 1999.

they feel accurate? You better believe it. They are as vivid and real as if a big meteorite were about to turn you into powder. Once again, your emotions are off the mark.

You must learn that emotions are just that—emotions. They are a product of your beliefs. And not only of your beliefs, but of your ongoing thoughts, what you dwell upon, what the Bible calls "meditations."

If you don't feel that great right now, ask yourself: "What have I been thinking?" If you are feeling guilty, ask yourself, "What have I been thinking about?" Stay on it until you figure it out. Don't let yourself feel vaguely uncomfortable or out of sorts with God; make yourself understand where those feelings came from. Check out their passport; they may be illegal aliens!

Guilty feelings can come from some thoughts you have, maybe from some thoughts you have a great deal of the time. Evaluate those thoughts for truth. Evaluate them according to what you know about God and God's grace...not how you feel. Bring the truth of God's word to bear on the subject. Hear me loud and clear on this: Just because you *feel* guilty, it doesn't mean you *are* guilty! Some of us have overactive, "weak" consciences that accuse us for no valid reason. We must re-train our consciences to go by the standard of the Bible. Don't be controlled by your feelings, but by the facts of what the Word says and by the standards it upholds.

Think new, different and better thoughts. Your feelings will change—perhaps not immediately, but change they will. They will obey your thoughts as surely as physical objects obey the law of gravity. They have to, and they always will. They change, not by you willfully, directly trying to change them, but by thinking about true things, better things, beautiful things, wonderful things.

Don't try to feel your way into a better way of feeling or a better way of acting. Instead, change your mind. Dwell upon other and better things. Occupy your mind with the things of God: the greatness of his promises and the wonder of his love, kindness and compassion. Your feelings will come around.

Changing your habits of thought, like changing any habit, is not easy. Do not be discouraged when you find that you have to work at it. We Guilty Souls have learned our negative thinking over long periods of practice, and it will not change without effort. But, since God has told us to set our minds (Colossians 3:1–4, Romans 8:5), this means that we can change even our most deeply ingrained thought patterns.[1]

Philippians 4:9 tells us to take action. Paul tells us to imitate the good things we see in his life: "Whatever you have learned or received or heard from me, or seen in me—put it into practice."

Just because we are saved by grace does not mean that action has no role in our lives. Paul here says that we are not only to think good thoughts, but that we are to do good things.

When we are not feeling especially mindful of grace, taking action can help us. Oftentimes our moods improve when we go out and serve God in some practical way. We need to help others. We can help someone else find Jesus, or we can encourage a fellow Christian. When our emotions become tangled and confused with guilt, we may need to simply do something positive and let those feelings die from lack of attention. Sometimes we just need to act ourselves into a better way of feeling. If we Guilty Souls become too analytical of our feelings

---

[1] Burns' book has excellent material on changing our thinking. Also, *Mind Change: The Overcomer's Handbook* (written by Thomas Jones and published by DPI) and *The Winning Attitude* (written by John Maxwell and published by Nelson) are great resources on this topic.

and thoughts, we can needlessly paralyze ourselves. What we may need is not more introspection, but a healthy dose of obedience and selfless service. We can decide what our motives will be and act on them in simple faith. After we have finished serving or sharing, we usually will find that the emotions that tormented us have dissipated or disappeared altogether.

I wonder if Paul and Silas felt a profound emotional sense of appreciation for God and his grace that night in the Philippian jail. They had been severely beaten, thrown in the stockade, and were bound with chains. I don't imagine they were all warm and giddy with a sense of overwhelming grace. But they sang anyway.

Was Jesus feeling warm and fuzzy about dying on the cross as he prayed to God in the garden of Gethsemane? I don't think so:

> Then Jesus went with his disciples to a place called Gethsemane, and he said to them, "Sit here while I go over there and pray." He took Peter and the two sons of Zebedee along with him, and he began to be sorrowful and troubled. Then he said to them, "My soul is overwhelmed with sorrow to the point of death. Stay here and keep watch with me." Going a little farther, he fell with his face to the ground and prayed, "My Father, if it is possible, may this cup be taken from me. Yet not as I will, but as you will."
>
> Then he returned to his disciples and found them sleeping. "Could you men not keep watch with me for one hour?" he asked Peter. "Watch and pray so that you will not fall into temptation. The spirit is willing, but the body is weak." (Matthew 26:36–41)

Jesus' feelings and desires were not in a great place at this moment. He was overwhelmed with sorrow. He was anxious. He did not want to do what God wanted him to do. He acknowledged his feelings and his will, and decided to obey

God. He did not go by his feelings, but he did acknowledge them. He did not do his own will, but he did acknowledge that he had one. He surrendered his feelings and his actions to his Father in a decision of will. He then arose from prayer and went on to face the horrible ordeal that lay before him.

Guilty Soul, you will many times have to do the same thing. This does not mean you are insincere. It does not mean your motives are evil or that you are a hypocrite. It simply means that you sometimes will have to bring your will and emotions into line with God's will by a decision—a decision to love God and others above yourself. This is not acting from the wrong motives. Instead, it is deciding to have the right motives. It is deciding to do the right thing in the face of fear, doubt and selfishness. It means you are a human being and that you will have to decide to take up the cross of self-denial many times, every day you live. But just remember to trust grace as you do.

Thankfully, not every day is supremely difficult. But when it is hard to obey, we can find the grace to help us. We will find that as we think what we should think and act in a way that pleases our Father in heaven, we mature. No longer are we controlled by our emotions, but we are controlled by the will and love of God. His grace has won our heart, and we give it to him regardless of how we may feel at the moment. And, in the long run, we find our emotions becoming more settled as we no longer live under their control, but under the Lordship of Christ.

Chapter 15

Grace and Commitment

> What then? Are we to sin because we are not under law but under grace? By no means! Do you not know that if you yield yourselves to anyone as obedient slaves, you are slaves of the one whom you obey, either of sin, which leads to death, or of obedience, which leads to righteousness? But thanks be to God, that you who were once slaves of sin have become obedient from the heart to the standard of teaching to which you were committed.
>
> Romans 6:15–17 (RSV)

God calls us to be committed to him. Jesus calls us to take our cross and follow him. How are we to understand this? Do these divine expectations undo all we have been saying about grace?

Grace Inspires Commitment

— the state or quality of being dedicated to a cause, activity

Whenever we are dearly loved, the natural response is to love in return. How is our love to be expressed? In commitment. Commitment is a way of returning love, of showing gratitude.

When I first met my wife, Geri, I found myself drawn to her. After coming to know her, I came to love her, and she came to love me. I wanted a permanent relationship with her.

But to have that relationship at the level of intimacy and trust that I desired, I realized that it would take commitment. I committed to her, and did so at a level greater than any other commitment I would ever make to another human being. I did so not to make her love me, but to enable me to have a lifetime relationship. I did not commit to Geri because I fell in love with commitment. I committed to Geri because I fell in love with *her.*

Can we begin to see it now? <u>Commitment gives us the capacity to be in a relationship</u>, <u>to be near to someone who loves us</u>. Our lack of commitment to God will not change his love for us, but it will keep us from being in a relationship with him.

Jesus loves everyone. Jesus loved the Pharisees just as much as he loved his closest disciples. They, however, did not love him in return and never had a relationship with him. Jesus cannot be close to anyone who will not return his love. Jesus loved his enemies, even those who persecuted him. After delivering a scathing rebuke to Jerusalem, Jesus grieved over the city, saying,

> "O Jerusalem, Jerusalem, you who kill the prophets and stone those sent to you, how often I have longed to gather your children together, as a hen gathers her chicks under her wings, *but you were not willing.*" (Matthew 23:37, emphasis mine)

The gift of love and grace is extended to all, but we must respond in love to possess it as our own.

Grace Defines Commitment

The depth of the grace that God gives determines our proper response. The only acceptable response to the grace of God is a total one. Oftentimes we would like the privileges of intimacy without the commitment that intimacy requires. We would like the blessings without the responsibilities. Jesus expects the greatest of all responses:

> Then he called the crowd to him along with his disciples and said: "If anyone would come after me, he must deny himself and take up his cross and follow me. For whoever wants to save his life will lose it, but whoever loses his life for me and for the gospel will save it. What good is it for a man to gain the whole world, yet forfeit his soul? Or what can a man give in exchange for his soul? If anyone is ashamed of me and my words in this adulterous and sinful generation, the Son of Man will be ashamed of him when he comes in his Father's glory with the holy angels." (Mark 8:34–38)

He expects us to respond to him more deeply than we do to any other person:

> "If anyone comes to me and does not hate his father and mother, his wife and children, his brothers and sisters—yes, even his own life—he cannot be my disciple. And anyone who does not carry his cross and follow me cannot be my disciple." (Luke 14:26–27)

Jesus expressed this calling another way, and perhaps in a more understandable way in relation to grace, when he said,

> "'Love the Lord your God with all your heart and with all your soul and with all your mind.' This is the first and greatest commandment." (Matthew 22:37–38)

Jesus offers us the greatest love we could ever know, the greatest love that has ever been offered to us. He expects and commands us to respond in kind.

Grace Is Consistent with Commitment

To some of us, Jesus' call for commitment seems like a withdrawal of the offer of grace. We read the fine print and feel there is a catch. We think this means the gospel is no longer free, that we are back into earning our way again: "Obey or else. I won't love you unless you do this for me."

Perhaps we will never be able to figure out all of this and make it fit exactly into a neat theological system. Perhaps God expects us to exercise a bit more common sense and to look at things more simply.

God loves us. He loved us before we loved him. He will always love us and will love us if we never respond, or if we respond and then turn our backs on him later. However, we must love him back in order to enjoy and experience his love, and to have a relationship with God. Our response must be more than mere intellectual acceptance. We respond with faith, which means we trust in God and his word above our own wisdom. It means obeying what God says. Without a trust that leads to obedience, our faith is not true Biblical faith (James 2:14–26).

Many people would like grace to provide them a free ride. They would like a "get out of jail free" card. They want a way to be forgiven but still live a life of sin, or of lukewarm, casual dedication. This is impossible. God sees through it and won't have it. God has written into the nature of things the law of response and reciprocation. He initiates, we respond. He gives, we give back. He provides, but we must believe.

Most Guilty Souls I know are people who are trying hard to be committed to Christ. They want to please God and want to obey him. They want to be used by him and want to help others. They just can't seem to understand how much God loves them and how abundant is the supply of grace available to help them. They will read the words of the Scriptures that call for commitment and feel overwhelmed and inadequate. Instead, they need to understand them properly.

Others, however, will hear the message of grace and, with a yawn, think, "Sure, God loves me. I'm pretty great. I have my weaknesses, but doesn't everybody? Surely God is not going to take them so seriously. Surely I don't have to be deeply committed and dedicated. I just need to believe in God and in Jesus, and that is enough. Some people (like the guilty guy who wrote this book) really need to be, and ought to be, super dedicated. But that's not for me or for most people. I don't see the point in getting all worked up about the commitment thing."

But Guilty Souls respond as we may have done when we were a kid back in school. We were the good kids who tried hard. But there were some other kids in class who could have cared less. They disrespected the teacher and neglected their studies. The teacher disciplined them and may have even become angry with them. Sometimes the whole class got in trouble because of them.

In situations like this, the "good kid" can take this rebuke the wrong way. They may think the teacher is mad at them, just like at the "bad kids." The good kid sometimes does wrong and needs correction, but he usually responds better to a different kind of leadership. He needs more affirmation, encouragement and reassurance. The corrections that bounce off the hardheaded, hardhearted kids, hit the good kid with painful intensity. He needs to learn that the strong corrections were needed to get someone else's attention. Therefore, a good rule of thumb, Guilty Souls, when we read some of the more challenging passages in the Scriptures, is to ask, "To whom was this spoken and why?"

Grace Enables Commitment

Commitment to Christ is enabled by the grace of God. Commitment is a decision we make, but the ability to keep that commitment comes by grace. We Guilty Souls often compartmentalize God's work. We may come to believe that we are forgiven by grace, but that we are left on our own when it comes to living the Christian life. Not true! Paul writes to Timothy (who was probably a Guilty Soul), "You then, my son, be strong in the grace that is in Christ Jesus" (2 Timothy 2:1). Grace not only saves us from the guilt of sin, but also from the power of sin. We are given the Holy Spirit to strengthen us. We are promised God's help through prayer. We are not on our own!

Commitment is essential. Commitment is vital. God loves us whether we commit or not, but without committing our lives to Christ, we cannot have a relationship with God.

As Christians, the more we grow in that commitment, the closer to God we can be and the more we can enjoy a deepening fellowship of love. But God loves no one more than anyone else. He is the perfect parent who loves his children all the same. Some kids may be closer because they are more mature or because they are more obedient, but all are equally loved.

So, be committed! Be committed as a way to show your love and as a way to respond to grace. Be committed as a way to be nearer to God and to be used more effectively by him. Remember that your level of commitment will not make God love you more, though it may make him more pleased. And as we grow in our commitment, we will grow closer to God and even more aware of how needful we are of his amazing grace.

In his famous hymn, Isaac Watts sums up what our

response should be to the gracious sacrifice of our Father and
his Son:

> When I survey the wondrous cross,
> on which the prince of glory died,
> my richest gain I count but loss,
> and pour contempt on all my pride.
>
> Forbid it, Lord, that I should boast,
> save in the death of Christ, my Lord:
> All the vain things that charm me most,
> I sacrifice them to his blood.
>
> See, from His head, His hands,
> His feet, sorrow and love flow mingled down;
> Did e'er such love and sorrow meet,
> or thorns compose so rich a crown?
>
> Were the whole realm of nature mine,
> that were a present far too small;
> Love so amazing, so divine,
> demands my soul, my life, my all.

Chapter 16

Grace and Repentance

> When they heard this, they had no further objections and praised God, saying, "So then, God has granted even the Gentiles repentance unto life."
>
> Acts 11:18

> Those who oppose him he must gently instruct, in the hope that God will grant them repentance leading them to a knowledge of the truth.
>
> 2 Timothy 2:25

> After John was put in prison, Jesus went into Galilee, proclaiming the good news of God. "The time has come," he said. "The kingdom of God is near. Repent and believe the good news!"
>
> Mark 1:14–15

Just what is repentance? It is a change, a turning. Repentance is a change of mind. It is a change of heart. It is a change of will. It is a change of behavior, of life.

Jesus said that without repentance we perish (Luke 13:5).

How is it related to grace? If we are saved by grace, not by our deeds, how is it that repentance is required of us?

First, repentance is a gift of grace. God must help us to change. He helps us change our minds. In some way, God can help us change our minds and still leave us with free will. I do

↳ You are an amazing God.

68

not venture to say that I completely understand how God does this, but I can say that I fully accept it. Where the work of God to change us begins and ends, and where our responsibility to change ourselves begins and ends will always be a mystery and a paradox. It is one of those teachings in the Scriptures that we can get at, but perhaps never fully comprehend.

It is true that without free will, our humanity is removed, and we are no more than machines or animals. But it is also true that without God's grace, we cannot be saved, and there is no amount of good deeds we can do, or willpower we can muster, to please God and earn our salvation. We cannot figure out all of the details of how it works. Too much arguing from theory can get us confused. Recognizing our intellectual limitations, we need to bring all the Scriptures to bear on this difficult subject and come away with a balanced and Biblical view.

Paul says in 2 Timothy 2:25 that for someone trapped in sin, there is hope—the hope that God will grant them repentance. Part of the trap of sin is the deception that goes with it: we do not see our sin, we minimize it and rationalize it. We need help to recognize our sin and to see a way out of it. God can give that. God, through his Spirit, can open our minds to see our sin. Like the prodigal son, we can come to our senses and see our condition (Luke 15:17). Like Lydia, God can open our hearts to the message (Acts 16:14). So, do we do this, or does God? The answer is that both of us do. We are *responsible* to seek repentance and make our own decision, or we are robots or machines. But we are also *dependent* on God's grace in seeking repentance and making our decision, or we are self-made and do not need mercy.

Here is another helpful verse:

> Therefore, my dear friends, as you have always
> obeyed—not only in my presence, but now much
> more in my absence—continue to work out your sal-
> vation with fear and trembling, for it is God who
> works in you to will and to act according to his good
> purpose. (Philippians 2:12–13)

Paul seemed to have no problem urging us to do things for ourselves, with the clear understanding that we need God's help to do them. Maybe we make it too complicated. Perhaps we should simply work hard, all the while depending on grace to help, empower and bless. Ultimately, it is more God's grace than our effort, but God still wants us to decide and make an effort. Yet, in some way, he can and does give us the added willpower we need to repent. Confused? I hope not. Just trust it, try it, and let God work it all out.

It is by grace that God lets us repent or accepts us when we do.

When at the Jerusalem conference the early church stated, "God has granted the Gentiles repentance unto life" (Acts 11:18), they recognized that it was God who graciously gives the ability and the opportunity to repent. God's acceptance of repentance is an act of grace. Why should he accept it, after all we have done to offend and hurt him? Is he in some way obligated to us? Does our repentance pay him back for the price paid on the cross? Instinctively we know this is not true. Instead we realize that God accepts, counts and reckons our repentance in a gracious manner. He graciously looks upon us as we repent.

So, is repentance necessary? Of course it is. God says so. Does repentance earn us anything, or does it place God in our debt? No, it does not.

In summary:

> Repentance is a gift from God.
> Repentance is our gift to God.
> Repentance is required by God.
> Repentance is enabled by God.
> Repentance is graciously accepted by God.
> Repentance is a decision for which we are personally responsible, but which God assists and enables.

If we desire to change, God will help us to change. God can and will move in our hearts, increasing our willpower and desire to grow and overcome. Let us seek repentance, knowing that even here, God graciously helps us and that we are not alone. → But we must believe that he will do this for us.

Chapter 17

Grace and Baptism

But when the kindness and love of God our Savior appeared, he saved us, not because of righteous things we had done, but because of his mercy. He saved us through the washing of rebirth and renewal by the Holy Spirit, whom he poured out on us generously through Jesus Christ our Savior, so that, having been justified by his grace, we might become heirs having the hope of eternal life.

Titus 3:4–7

"And now what are you waiting for? Get up, be baptized and wash your sins away, calling on his name."

Acts 22:16

Baptism is an experience of grace. It is the moment, when in faith and in response to God's love and calling, we enter into union with Christ. It is the moment when, by the blood shed for us and by the love given to us, God reaches down and saves us. It is when we are born again of water and the Spirit. It is when our sins are washed away, when we are cleansed. It is when we are transferred from darkness into the light. It is when we are added to God's church and incorporated into his family. It is an unforgettable, unrepeatable, glorious and earth-shaking moment.

Baptism is not primarily something we do for God, but something God does for us, and in us. We respond in faith and submit in faith, and without our willingness, baptism is meaningless. But it is far more than what *we* do. It is what God does. He is the one who at that moment imparts to us the righteousness of Jesus. He is the one who has ordained that at that moment and in that way he unites us with Christ.

Baptism is an experience of grace. In it we are not trusting in ourselves or in our deeds, but in the mercy and kindness of God and in the deeds of Jesus. We are looking to the cross, not to ourselves.

Baptism should not be construed as our work, but as the work of God. Baptism is something we decide to submit to, but the power of it comes from God and from the work of Jesus on the cross. Like Paul, we get up and are baptized, and as we do, we call upon Jesus' name to save us. By "the name" the Scriptures refer to all that is contained in the character, goodness, righteousness and mercy of Christ. We look to him, not to ourselves. We are drawing on an account of righteousness that is owned by Another, whose payment of the price of sins comes from the riches of his grace. If we go to our own account to pay our debt, we come up abysmally short. We are bankrupt of the funds of righteousness to pay the debt we owe. His account, however, is limitless. His goodness, his blood, his mercy are unfailing.

There is no question that the early Christians understood their baptism to be the moment of forgiveness, marking the beginning point of their walk with Jesus. It was the moment they could look back to as their birthday, the time when by grace they were born again. It was for them a supreme memory of grace.

(margin note: "Do not let sin be your master" v.14)

When Paul says, "Don't you not know" in Romans 6:3, it is as if he is saying, "Don't you remember? Don't you recall the moment when you began your Christian life? Don't you remember what you experienced as you were buried in the water? You were buried with Christ. By grace you experienced the death he died for you. By grace you died with him. His death was agonizing, painful and by it he became sin and bore your sin. Your death in baptism was by faith, by grace and because of grace; it was an experience of joy, sublime joy.

The fundamental message of Romans 6:1–14 is that in baptism we are united with Christ. It is the repetition of the prepositional phrases "into him," "with him" or "with Christ" that tell us why baptism is such a wonderful experience of grace. It is here that we are joined with Christ. We are in baptism connected to him, united with him. We are not alone when we enter the water. We experience his death both spiritually and graciously because we are given the benefits of what he accomplished, yet without having to actually experience the agonies that he did.

We are consistently pictured as being acted upon by God in baptism. Several key verbs in Romans 6:1–14 are in the passive voice. This means that the subject of the sentence is receiving the action of the verb rather than doing the acting. Note these examples: We were baptized into him and his death (v3), we were buried together with him through baptism into his death (v4), we were united with (or we shared with) him (v5), we were crucified with him (v6). Isn't that what grace is all about? In baptism, God acts for us and on our behalf, doing for us what we cannot do for ourselves.

In baptism we are not only buried with Christ, but we are also raised with him (vv4–5). We share his resurrection. As

Jesus was raised by the Spirit out of a physical and spiritual grave (Ephesians 1:19–20), so the Holy Spirit raises us out of a physical (water) and spiritual grave. Our experience is a spiritual one in that we are at that moment given the Holy Spirit, the Spirit who will now dwell in us. We have a new life before us, and we now have within us the power to live it. The Spirit was given to us by grace in the moment of our baptism, placed within the now cleansed temple of our bodies to dwell as a permanent resident (Acts 2:38, 1 Corinthians 3:16, 6:19).

We can look forward to the formidable challenge of changing our lives to conform to God's will with confidence, knowing we have his power, the power of the Holy Spirit, at our disposal. We are both cleansed and empowered at the moment of our baptism.

That is why Peter can say, "His divine power has given us everything we need for life and godliness" (2 Peter 1:3). It is why Paul can say that we have been blessed with "every spiritual blessing in Christ" (Ephesians 1:3). These blessings are already ours. They were given when we were born again, from the very first day of our walk with Jesus, when we were baptized into him. They are now ours for the taking, and we have a lifetime to learn how to tap into the gracious provision that God has made available to us.

Guilty Souls often devise reasons to doubt the validity of their baptism. We often dredge up one more sin that we neglected to confess or wonder if our motives were all they should have been. *Was I humble enough? Was I really broken? Did I appreciate grace enough? If I were a true Christian, I wouldn't struggle so much.* On and on we go. Continual doubt is eliminated when we have the proper understanding of baptism and grace.

Isn't it true that pride, imperfect motives, ingratitude and weakness are the reasons we need grace and baptism in the first place? If when we were baptized, we trusted in the cross of Jesus to save us, repented and made Jesus Lord, then we can be sure we experienced the "one baptism" (Ephesians 4:5) and that our salvation is secure. We can look back to our baptism with confidence, knowing that at that moment we were forgiven and born again. In time we mature spiritually and come to greater realization of our sin and the depth of Christ's sufferings, and a greater appreciation of grace. This is to be expected and should not cause us to doubt our original decision. There simply is no perfect baptism...except that of Jesus himself.

Look back to your baptism as a supreme experience of grace. Never forget what happened then. Never forget how it happened. It happened by grace. It was initiated by God, given meaning by him, and invested with power by him. You believed, you repented, you responded, you acted. But it was God who saved. It was God who called and enabled you, and it was he who, in those waters and at that time, reached down and saved you by his grace through what Jesus did for you on his cross and in his resurrection.

Chapter 18

Gifted by Grace

For it is by grace you have been saved, through faith—
and this not from yourselves, it is the gift of God—not
by works, so that no one can boast. For we are God's
workmanship, created in Christ Jesus to do good
works, which God prepared in advance for us to do.

Ephesians 2:8–10

For by the grace given me I say to every one of you:
Do not think of yourself more highly than you ought,
but rather think of yourself with sober judgment, in
accordance with the measure of faith God has given
you. Just as each of us has one body with many members, and these members do not all have the same
function, so in Christ we who are many form one
body, and each member belongs to all the others. We
have different gifts, according to the grace given us. If
a man's gift is prophesying, let him use it in proportion to his faith. If it is serving, let him serve; if it is
teaching, let him teach; if it is encouraging, let him
encourage; if it is contributing to the needs of others,
let him give generously; if it is leadership, let him gov-
ern diligently; if it is showing mercy, let him do it
cheerfully.

Romans 12:3–8

You are gifted. You may not think so. You may not feel so.
But the Bible says you are. "We have different gifts," Paul

says in the verse above. And in another place, he says,

> *But to each one of us grace has been given* as Christ
> apportioned it. This is why it says:
>
> "When he ascended on high,
>   he led captives in his train
>   and *gave gifts to men*."
> (Ephesians 4:7–8, emphasis mine)

what is my gift?

You were not forgotten when the gifts were handed out. You belong in the gifted class!

Romans 12:3 warns us against pride, against thinking we are greater than we are or that our abilities are given to us because we are deserving of them. We are what we are due to the grace of God. If you are arrogant and prideful, realize that all you have came from God. Do not overestimate yourself. Be realistic. Be sober in self-judgment, Paul says. Being sober means that we see ourselves realistically—not better than we are, or worse, but as we are.

Guilty Souls, however, often suffer from a low opinion of themselves and feel inadequate and lacking in ability. We are more likely to respond to God's calling in our lives in a manner similar to that of Moses:

> But Moses said to God, "Who am I, that I should go to
> Pharaoh and bring the Israelites out of Egypt?"...Moses
> said to the LORD, "O Lord, I have never been eloquent,
> neither in the past nor since you have spoken to your
> servant. I am slow of speech and tongue." (Exodus
> 3:11, 4:10)

It takes some doing for God to convince Moses he will be able to fulfill his calling. Moses has lost his confidence. He feels so incapable and unworthy that he still doubts, even when God himself reassures him and shows him miracles. He doubts that God can or will use him. He claims he has been a

I feel like I still doubt.

poor speaker from his youth. That flies in the face of his history: Stephen, telling Moses' story, says that as a young man Moses was "powerful in speech and action" (Acts 7:22). What has happened to this once confident man? Could it be that he has become a Guilty Soul? Has his shame over his murder of the Egyptian slave driver and the rejection by both his own people and the Egyptians broken his confidence? Quite likely, in the past his confidence had been in the wrong place—in himself and not in God. But now, he cannot even muster any confidence at all, even when God himself says he should have it.

Guilty Souls, many of us have had experiences like this. Perhaps we were once confident, but our confidence was in ourselves and not in God. Now we remember with shame our pride as we attempted to serve God in our own way and in our own power. We failed. We hurt others. We were embarrassed by our folly. We now think that God is done with us or that if we were to try to use whatever talent we have in God's service, his people would reject us. And so we, like Moses, sit in our own self-imposed exile, herding sheep in the middle of nowhere.

But God is gracious, and he will use us again. He can even use us in greater ways than we dreamed before. We need to accept forgiveness, and we need to recognize the gifts of grace with which God has equipped us for service. We bring no glory to God by refusing either.

What Are Your Gifts?

Let me give some practical helps to start you on a path of discovery. None of these alone is an infallible guide to discovering your gifts. But if you put them all together, they make a compelling case. As you begin, remember—*you are gifted*. The

Bible says so. No Christian is left out! Now, let's take a look
and see what we discover.

*a..Interpreting
art, body language
communicating
w/ people.*
b. Drawing/Painting
*c. Conversing
w/ woman.*
*I'm easy to talk
to.* (?)

1. *Your gift is something that you are good at.* You "get
it." You learn it quickly. You pick it up quicker than
most people. This does not preclude you working
to develop your proficiency, but it means your
efforts are blessed with success.

I have observed that when something comes
easy to us, we can take it for granted. We reason
that only those tasks that require immense sacrifice
or excruciating labor are truly "spiritual." We also
think that if we do something we enjoy, we are
being self-indulgent. "Where is the sacrifice?" we
say. This is typical of the Guilty Soul's convoluted
thinking. Just because a skill comes relatively easy
does not mean that it is not a gift of God. (In fact,
if it comes relatively easy, it most likely is a gift
from God.) Nor should we think that it is unspiritual to enjoy using that gift in God's service. *← I feel this
way some-
times.*

2. *Others comment and are blessed when you use your
gift.* Do other people notice and feel encouraged
when you involve yourself in a particular ministry
or activity? Then that probably means it is a gift
God has given you. If, on the other hand, others do
not respond positively, then this may be telling you
that your gifts lie elsewhere.

3. *Spiritual leaders encourage you in the use of your gift.*
God gives leaders the responsibility to help develop
and equip members of the body of Christ to use their
talents and abilities (Ephesians 4:12). If spiritual

leaders see a gift you have and encourage you to use and develop it, see this as another piece of the puzzle coming together.

4. *You are fulfilled when you use your gift.* You have a sense of "this is what I was meant to do. This is where I feel the most like myself. This is the real me." I am reminded of the words of the missionary Eric Liddle in the film *Chariots of Fire*, who, in commenting on his running ability said, "I believe God made me for a purpose—for China. But he also made me *fast*. And when I run, I feel his pleasure." Take pleasure in using the gifts God has graciously bestowed upon you; the enjoyment you feel is a part of the blessing your Father in heaven intends you to feel!

We must realize that no one of these tests is absolutely reliable. Our own confidence may be so low and we may be so self-conscious that we cannot evaluate ourselves accurately. We might not see how gifted we really are.

On the other hand, we might think we are more gifted than we are. This is where other people can help us evaluate and use our gifts.

Remember too, spiritual leaders sometimes miss the mark as to who has what gift. They are imperfect and have their own blind spots and prejudices that could cause them not to recognize your abilities. Or they may think you are capable of more than you are and could mistakenly select you to do something you are not equipped or ready to do. Continue to seek God's guidance in realizing and using your gifts.

Some of us worry that we could become so wrapped up in using our gifts that God gets crowded out of the picture. We fear that our pride could take over and that our gift could become an idol to us. This is a real possibility. To keep this from happening, we must remain grateful and humble, remembering that our abilities and opportunities are given by grace. We must strive to do what we do for the honor of God and for the benefit of others. Then we can take satisfaction in the knowledge that God has gifted us and is using us for the good of others and for his glory.

That being said, it is vital for Guilty Souls to remember that none of us will ever be perfectly motivated. Even at our most humble moments, pride and selfishness can creep into our thinking, and we may begin to feel superior or take too much credit. We may become envious of others or resentful when someone else is given a place of prominence. This is a temptation for every servant of the Lord, and if we all withdrew from serving because we struggle in this way, then nothing would ever get done! We need to confess any of these thoughts to the Lord, and to godly friends as well. In the meantime, let us give ourselves fully in serving the Lord, allowing him to discipline and mature us along the way.

It may take a while for you to find and develop your gifts. They may be buried under such inferiority feelings, failure or sin that it may take time to unearth them. Pray about it and ask the help of others. Experiment. Step out in faith. Don't worry if you make a few missteps. Strive to have pure motives, pray and go for it! Let God direct you. You may start out in one direction and end up at a polar opposite, or you may find that you were headed in the right direction all along, but needed time and experience to sharpen your focus.

If God gave you your gifts, don't you think that he would want you to discover and use them? Pray, and trust him for his grace to guide and instruct you. Study the passages on this topic.[1] Read some good books on the subject. Consult trusted friends, and listen to spiritual leaders.

Remember this: you will never feel deeply contented or useful until you are functioning in the body of Christ in your area of giftedness. This is God's plan. He wants you to be used. You are needed. You are important. You are not only saved by grace, you are gifted by grace.

You are God's workmanship. God is the master artisan, the sculptor, the painter, the inventor. You are the object of his thoughts, imagination and efforts. He is working to refine, equip, empower and enable you. He had something in mind when he created you, and he is moving to bring that design into being. He is the primary worker. You may not feel that way; it may seem it is mostly you making the effort and that there is just a little bit of God in there—*not true!*

You have a unique purpose, a unique design. You are like no one else. You are you, and you have a special place in your Father's heart and in his plan. You don't know exactly what his plans are, and neither does anyone else. He may have thus far given some general pointers, but the specifics he will reveal in time. They will probably surprise you. They will most certainly fulfill you. They will also be a source of blessing to those around you.

We have a deep need to be useful. We have an undefined yearning for significance and for a sense that our life is going somewhere, that it matters. Grace will see to it that those cravings are satisfied, that those needs are met, that our lives

---

[1] Exodus 35:30–36:1, Romans 12:3–8, 1 Corinthians 12, 1 Peter 4:7–11 will get you started.

Is my gift artistic craftsmenship ?

are used in a meaningful way. Grace does not save us just to get us to heaven. Grace equips and uses us for great works; we can serve in ways we never imagined.

I'm excited for you as you discover and use the gifts God has given you!

Chapter 19

Godly Sorrow, Worldly Sorrow

Even if I caused you sorrow by my letter, I do not regret it. Though I did regret it—I see that my letter hurt you, but only for a little while—yet now I am happy, not because you were made sorry, but because your sorrow led you to repentance. For you became sorrowful as God intended and so were not harmed in any way by us. Godly sorrow brings repentance that leads to salvation and leaves no regret, but worldly sorrow brings death. See what this godly sorrow has produced in you: what earnestness, what eagerness to clear yourselves, what indignation, what alarm, what longing, what concern, what readiness to see justice done. At every point you have proved yourselves to be innocent in this matter.

2 Corinthians 7:8-11

There is a proper sorrow or remorse we should feel. The presence of grace does not mean that we should never feel guilt for our sins. But how do we approach this? The Guilty Soul feels guilt, but too much, too often and too long. The Guilty Soul is dominated by what Paul calls "worldly sorrow."

The way this passage has often been explained is that worldly sorrow is basically regret that you got caught. For example, a policeman stops you when you are speeding. Your inner response is, *I sure am sorry he was patrolling this road today. This means a big fine and a higher insurance payment.* Obviously, this is not godly sorrow that you have broken the law, endangered other people, or in your pride felt you were above the law.

Although this is a valid interpretation of what Paul is saying here, I think it is equally dangerous that a Guilty Soul can experience worldly sorrow as destructive and excessive feelings of guilt. This was Paul's concern after the offending sinner was disciplined by the Corinthian church: "Now instead, you ought to forgive and comfort him, so that he will not be overwhelmed by excessive sorrow" (2 Corinthians 2:7). Worldly sorrow leaves out the grace of God. Worldly sorrow crushes with remorse and leaves the soul forlorn, with a sense of failure, worthlessness and hopelessness. If not corrected, it can lead to serious spiritual problems, even to spiritual death.

Perhaps the best way to understand the difference between proper and improper feelings of guilt is to consider the example of Judas and Peter. They both sinned against Jesus on the night of his arrest. Both men acted with cowardice, weakness and compromise. It is true that Judas' actions were premeditated, deliberate and treacherous. But consider the actions of Peter. He was warned that he would fail, and in his pride he said he would not. He denied he knew Jesus, and according to the Gospel accounts he had time to think about it before he denied Jesus a second and third time. He did what he did with full knowledge that it was wrong and after receiving a warning that he arrogantly dismissed.

Judas was gripped with remorse after his sin. He recognized he was wrong and that Jesus was innocent. He attempted to make amends. He took the money back and admitted his error to those with whom he had collaborated. He felt terrible sorrow, shame and guilt—as well he should have. He then went out and hung himself.

Peter also felt shame. As his words of denial rang out across the courtyard of the High Priest's home, the Scripture says that "the Lord turned and looked straight at Peter" (Luke 22:61). Peter remembered the words Jesus had spoken to him earlier and "went outside and wept bitterly" (Luke 22:62).

I would offer that these two men's responses to their sin, shame and failure illustrate the difference between godly sorrow and worldly sorrow.

Judas felt guilt, but would not accept grace. He felt intensely the shame of his betrayal and came to see how wrong he was. But he stopped short of seeing that in spite of his sin, there was a way of repentance and forgiveness. He took his own life before seeing or accepting that Jesus' death on the cross could have completely resolved his problem. He did not turn to Jesus for the grace he needed in his hour of sin and failure. Did he fail because of his pride or perhaps because of a hardened heart? Both are entirely possible, and Judas is completely responsible for his sin. But we also know that although he felt sorrow and saw the utter sin and selfishness of his actions, he would not face Jesus, and he would not let God forgive him.

Peter felt shame as well. Could he ever forget the eyes of Jesus penetrating into his soul at the moment of his denial? Could he ever forget the cowardliness of his actions and the pride with which he had scoffed at the possibility of ever being so weak? He abandoned his friend and Lord in the hour of his greatest need. His vaunted manhood lay in ruins. His professed faith and courage were but empty bluster. He was not the strong, faithful disciple he wanted to be or that he had believed himself to be.

Two men failed, and both felt shame. The outcome was different. One took his shame to the grave; the other took his shame to God.

How about you? Would you have had godly sorrow? When you sin, you need to see how it hurts God. See how it hurts Jesus. Do not hide your sin, but take it to God. Take it to God, not just to other people. Take it to God, not just to yourself. Confess it. Agree with God about it. If tears come, let them flow. Decide to change. "Godly sorrow leads to repentance." Repentance is a decision to change. It is both a realization of wrong and a commitment to be different. You cannot undo what you have done, but you can be forgiven, and you can be restored. There is no sin so great that God will not forgive it. Peter was forgiven, and Judas could have been forgiven as well.

When you have seen your sin and confessed, then let God forgive you. Go back and face the Lord, just as Peter did in John 21. You will find that while he wants you to repent, he will also forgive you and restore you to a place of usefulness. When Jesus said to Peter, "Feed my lambs" and "Take care of my sheep" (John 21:15–17), it is as if Jesus was saying, "Yes, you failed me, but you still love me, and I still love you. You are forgiven. I will give you a great purpose. Find that purpose in serving others. Help, care for, and nurture them. Protect my people. You failed me, but your failure is not final. I still have a role for you. It is not found in misery and self-loathing, but in serving. Get up, and get about the work I have for you to do."

If you are today living in despair and hopelessness over your past sins and present besetting sins, you need to have godly sorrow, not worldly sorrow. You do neither God nor yourself any good by hating, loathing and punishing yourself. Confess your sin to God and to others, and go on with your life. Otherwise, Jesus died in vain to free you from your bondage to sin and guilt.

When you struggle again with your weaknesses, do not return to your old habit of worldly sorrow. Realize that even with your highest intentions to never fail God again, you will. Even the most earnest Christians try and fall short. We may long for the ideal of perfect obedience, but it is not promised us. We may desire complete victory over our sins, but we must realize that life as a Christian is about growth, not about perfection.

The example of Peter once again enlightens us. He recovered from his earlier failure and went on to be a great servant of Jesus. He faced persecution with unflinching courage and bore bold testimony to his Lord. But there is more to Peter's story. Years later his old weakness returned. Under pressure he compromised and backed away from fellowshipping with his Gentile brothers. He gave in to fear again, wanting to please men rather than God. And he seemingly didn't even realize his error—Paul had to call him down in public (Galatians 2:11–21). How embarrassing! What a disappointing failure for the supposedly reformed, mature leader of God's people!

It is not that Peter lived a life of continual hypocrisy. It is not that he was a phony Christian or a charlatan. It is that he was a human being. It is that he was beset with weakness, and like all of us, if he did not stay close to his Lord, he could sin very easily. Like him, we all fail. And like him, we can fail in the same manner as we did in the past.

So, Guilty Soul, learn to have godly sorrow. When you sin, confess it and repent. Take your sin to God. Do not rationalize or cover up. Confess it to others as well. But when you have confessed, leave it with God. Do not allow guilty feelings to remain on your conscience. Do not allow them to separate you from your Father in heaven. Do not think you are worthless. Do not let your sins lead you to despair and hopelessness. And do not let guilt be your motivation to serve God. Let the fact that you have been freed of guilt be your motivation.

You do not deserve grace, but God has chosen to freely give it to you. You do not honor God or help yourself by having destructive, worldly sorrow. Let it go. Let God forgive you and restore you to a great purpose. And let him do it every time you fail.

Chapter 20

What Advantage to Always Feeling Guilty?

> He will not always accuse,
>   nor will he harbor his anger forever; *God doesn't stay angry forever.*
> he does not treat us as our sins deserve
> or repay us according to our iniquities.
>
> Psalm 103:9–10

If God forgives so freely, why do we stay in the state of feeling guilty? Why would we do so even when we know, intellectually at least, that we are fully forgiven?

I have some ideas.

First, Guilty Souls do not trust themselves to be strong without the threat of guilt.[1] Something within us makes us think that we must punish ourselves if we are to be, and remain, righteous and devoted. I suppose we differ with God, who says that love from him and for him is the most lasting and empowering motive there is. Guilty Souls think otherwise. We think that if we let the beast of Self off the hook and out of the cage, we are done for. We feel there is within us something so malevolent, so evil, so utterly selfish, that it can

---

[1] I am indebted to David Burns' observations on this subject in chapter 8 of *Feeling Good, The New Mood Therapy.*

91

be tamed only by caging and by our remaining perpetually uncomfortable, lest the monster escape and lead us to our ruin.

Let me ask you a question. When is the last time that believing that you were completely forgiven and loved by God caused you to go out on a binge of unbridled sin? Come on now, think about it. I am looking hard within myself right now, and I can't think of a single time in my life. "Ah, but it could happen," you say. "I would never want to become one of those cheap grace people." Well, neither would I, but I maintain that Guilty Souls are probably the last ones who would end up in that crowd. "Yes, and it's because I am hard on myself that I don't," you say. I respectfully disagree. I say that if you allowed yourself to enjoy your forgiveness, if you celebrated your salvation and delighted in God, your degree of holiness and righteousness would not decrease at all, but would instead increase.

You are going to have to trust God on this one. Trust that he knows you better than you know yourself. Trust that he knows better how to motivate and inspire than you do. Trust that if God wanted to keep you in jail to prevent you from being a spiritual criminal, he would have told you so. We are going to have to get used to the fact that God has given us our freedom—freedom from the penalty of sin and freedom, therefore, from the worst prison of all: a guilty conscience.

Another reason we stay guilt-ridden is to pay for our sins. We think it's just not right to be forgiven so freely, so quickly. We figure we need to pay our dues. We want to feel some misery, and enough of it to satisfy God, or ourselves at least. Tell me this: How long will you need to punish yourself? When will it be enough? When will the debt be satisfied? How will you know that it is? Has God let you in on something that he has never talked about in the Word? How intense does your suffering need to be to pay off your debt? Is there some magic communication that happens where you somehow know, "Okay, I have paid for my sin now. I have felt bad enough for long enough. I can now go free."

When we do this we become like Rodrigo Mendoza, the character from the film *The Mission*. Mendoza, an 18th century slave trader, kills his brother in a fit of rage, and in bitter remorse seeks to pay for his sin. He repeatedly attempts, in a driving rainstorm, to drag the heavy, cumbersome burden of his bundled up armor to the summit of a steep mountain. Each time he nears his goal, he is overcome, slips and falls back down to the bottom. What a picture of futility and failure! Can you relate? When we try to do penance, to pay the price of our own sins, we can never succeed. We will be driven to say with Mendoza, "There is no redemption, no penance great enough."

The truth is that there is no advantage to always feeling guilty, always feeling out of sorts with God, always feeling there is something wrong—not when you have learned the truth about Jesus and your sin, and have committed your life to God.

The only advantage is to the devil. You are so worried and fretful, so plain worn out from feeling guilty that it makes his job easier. You are certainly less of a threat to him and his kingdom since your guilt makes you more vulnerable to temptation and discouragement. Always feeling guilty and seeking ways to do penance will ultimately weaken your resistance to sin.

God's plan is freedom, yours is slavery and condemnation.

Choose his plan. God is smarter than you and knows best how to form you into who he wants you to be. He knows what will make you flourish and prosper spiritually. His way is the way of sunlight, joy and freedom, not of confinement, chains and guilt.

Why don't you try a little experiment? Let yourself off the hook for a while, and see what happens. Try it for an hour. Just for an hour. Let yourself out of jail, and walk around outside the prison walls like a free person. You can even leave the door open so you can run back inside if you find yourself heading into a life of self-indulgence. If you survive that hour, try it for an afternoon, then for a whole day. Just go out to the halfway house for a while. Then, finally, let yourself be fully free. Let yourself live as a beloved child, not as a prisoner or a slave. I'll make a bet with you. I bet you will be fine. You will be responsible. You will be righteous. You will stay that way. And you'll be a whole lot happier in the meantime.

Chapter 21

Grace and Self-Rejection

> How great is the love the Father has lavished on us,
> that we should be called children of God! And that is
> what we are!
>
> 1 John 3:1

Conviction of sin is not the same thing as rejecting your-self. Hating your sin does not mean you should hate yourself. Seeing how selfish you are does not mean that you come to believe that you are worthless.

We get really confused here. We think that to truly see our sin means we must feel that we are utterly worthless in God's eyes. If that is so, then what do the Scriptures mean when they say we were created in the image of God? What does David mean when he says we are a little lower than the angels? If we were not worth something, why would Jesus have bothered to die for us?

You might ask, "Didn't Jesus say we are to hate our lives?" (Luke 14:26). In this passage he is laying out the need for us to establish spiritual priorities. We are not to live selfish lives. We are to never let our desire to direct our own lives or to pro-tect ourselves make us shy away from giving our lives com-pletely to Christ. Jesus in this same verse also says we are to hate our closest relatives. He means by this that our love for them should never come before our love for him and our commitment to God. He cannot mean that we are to be malicious to, disdain or resent our family since he has told us to love our neighbor as ourselves (Matthew 22:29).

Likewise, we are not to disdain or resent ourselves, but keep ourselves in proper relation to God. We are to never exalt ourselves and our will to the position of supremacy reserved for God alone. Paradoxically, when we put selfish desires above Jesus, we actually lose our true Self (Luke 9:23–25). (See also John 12:25, Matthew 10:37–39 as parallel references.)

The truth is that we are worth infinitely much in the eyes of God. He cares for us. He delights in us. He longs for a relationship with us. He made us in his image. He made us for fellowship with himself. God does not hate us; he hates our sin.

Our sin is deeply a part of us, but as author John Eldredge says, "Sin is not the deepest thing about [us]." The deepest thing about us is that we are made by God and that we are made in his image.[1]

We should hate our sin for the offense that it is to God. We should hate it for what it did to Jesus and for the grief it causes God. We should hate it for what it does to others and for what it has done to us as well. But we should not hate *ourselves*. When we see sin in ourselves, we should deal with it. We should confess it and repent of it. But we should reject our sin and not reject ourselves. If God, though he sees our sin far more vividly than we, does not hate us, why should we hate ourselves?

Some of us are so disturbed by our sin and selfishness that

a good question (because of the guilt and shame of God seeing our sin.

---

[1]John Eldredge, *Wild at Heart* (Nashville: Nelson, 2001), 134.

we loathe ourselves. We feel that to like ourselves or to feel good about ourselves is a form of self-worship. But we are wrong. Regarding ourselves as beloved of God and made in his image, is not pride or self-worship: it is spiritual reality. Recognizing the truth that apart from God we lapse into self-ishness is a wise thing. We can give in to pride very easily. But to be forever ill at ease and to think that self-affirmation and a sense of contentment, peace and security in our salvation are signs of pride is a wrong-headed conception.

Let God love you. Learn to be glad that God made you the way he did. Your gifts, abilities, talents, capacities all come from God. They are to be recognized, enjoyed, celebrated, acknowledged and used for God's glory. Paul knew his sin. He declared that he was the worst of sinners (1 Timothy 1:15–16). But he said more than that: he said that he was something, and somebody, by the grace of God (1 Corinthians 15:10). If it is true for Paul, why not for you and me?

Paul is a great example of someone who acknowledged God's glory and grace.

Paul calls himself the worst of sinners. He then says "But for that very reason, I was shown mercy so that in me Christ Jesus might display his unlimited patience..." 1 Timothy 1:16

God gives us mercy, glory, grace and so much more because he LOVES us.

God made me this way and my talents are to be used for God's glory.

Chapter 22

Desperate for Grace

Have mercy on me, O God,
    according to your unfailing love;
according to your great compassion
    blot out my transgressions.

Psalm 51:1

David was a man after God's own heart. He loved God dearly and deeply. As I have read about his life and studied his magnificent psalms, I have found myself both inspired and shamed (there I go again!) by what I have seen. Here is a man who loved and knew God so intimately and so passionately that his words and life move us after thousands of years. Here is a man who, though he lived before the time of the cross, seemed to understand grace better than many of us who have known for years the message of Jesus and his gospel.

But David sinned. He sinned deliberately, with forethought and malice. He transgressed viciously, deceitfully and manipulated his friends to assist him in his sin. He committed adultery with Bathsheba, the wife of his trusted friend Uriah, whom he ordered to be murdered to cover up his transgression. In spite of the enormity of his crimes, David did not come to repent of his wrong because of a tender conscience; it took a prophet's courageous confrontation to bring him to his senses.

How could this be? How could a man so close to God do such heinous things? Perhaps we will never fully understand, but we must with godly fear acknowledge that all of us are sinners and are capable of the most horrible of crimes. I agree

Perhaps most importantly of all, we can learn not only how a righteous man can sin, but how a good heart repents. Do I have a good heart?

Let us look at David's great prayer of repentance: Psalm 51. I often use this psalm to guide my prayers and thoughts during times of repentance.

In the opening passage, David appeals to God for mercy. He does so not on the basis of the goodness or greatness of his sorrow, but on the basis of the compassion and unfailing love of God.

In our effort to repent, Guilty Souls often focus upon the degree of guilt we can feel as the basis of our appeal to God. This is the wrong focus. The focus should be upon the compassion and unfailing love of God, not upon how great is our sorrow. To focus on that is to depend not upon grace, but upon our sorrow and our penitence as the means of forgiveness.

Could David have ever grieved enough to make God forgive him? Would that bring back Uriah, restore Bathsheba's honor, or efface the guilt of the crime he ordered Joab to commit? The basis of forgiveness is God's love and mercy, not our feelings of guilt. If we focus here, we are headed for either a hardened heart or a life of never knowing if we are forgiven. There are not enough tears we can cry or enough shame we can feel to earn our way to the cleansing of our souls. very true

> Wash away all my iniquity
> and cleanse me from my sin. (Psalm 51:2)

David here openly appeals for cleansing of his sin. He

asks for washing, for purification. Sin is like a stain on our souls. It is dirt on our consciences, filth on our hearts. We can only ask for it to be taken away.

> For I know my transgressions,
>   and my sin is always before me.
> Against you, you only, have I sinned
>   and done what is evil in your sight,
> so that you are proved right when you speak
>   and justified when you judge.
> Surely I was sinful at birth,
>   sinful from the time my mother conceived me.
> (Psalm 51:3–5)

David openly acknowledges his sin. He confesses it. It is always before him. He is not trying to escape it or minimize it. He recognizes that his sin is fundamentally against God. He does not mean to say that he did not sin against others, but he simply admits that the vertical issue of sin is far more significant than the horizontal. Ultimately, all sin is against God. When we sin against another person, we also sin against God himself. David then says, in essence, "God, you are right. I am a sinner. There is no excuse. You are totally correct in your judgment." There is no blaming of Bathsheba, no saying, "What about Joab?" no mention of any mitigating circumstances: "What about all the pressure I was under? It was just a moment of weakness." No rationalization. None.

> Surely you desire truth in the inner parts;
>   you teach me wisdom in the inmost place.
> (Psalm 51:6)

David now acknowledges another need: for deep truthfulness in his inner self. Sin is always accompanied by some sort of deception. Even if we do not directly deceive others, in some way we are deceived by Satan, or we deceive our-

[handwritten margin note:] There are times when I recognize that my sin hurts God and I appologize & ask for forgiveness.

[handwritten note:] VERY TRUE!

Do I love the truth?

selves. If we would be clear of sin, we must become lovers of truth. Only the acknowledgment of truth in the deepest levels of our souls can help us deal with sin as we should. David in the NIV translation says God desires and teaches us "truth in the inner parts" and "the inmost place." But is this not also a prayer for God to do this very thing? It is a similar prayer to one that he prayed at another time:

> Search me, O God, and know my heart;
>   test me and know my anxious thoughts.
> See if there is any offensive way in me,
>   and lead me in the way everlasting.
> (Psalm 139:23–24)

I've been tested on my anxious thoughts, I believe

and another:

> Who can discern his errors?
>   Forgive my hidden faults.
> Keep your servant also from willful sins;
>   may they not rule over me.
> Then will I be blameless,
>   innocent of great transgression.
> May the words of my mouth and the meditation of
>   my heart
>   be pleasing in your sight,
> O LORD, my Rock and my Redeemer.
> (Psalm 19:12–14)

David wants to see what he has done. He wants to know how selfish and sinful it was. He is not evading the truth. He is not running from God. He is not hiding, as did Adam and Eve. He comes to God in the midst of his shame and sin and in effect says: "God, I have sinned. But I want to see it. I want to see it like you do. I want more than head knowledge. I want heart knowledge. I want to see it like you see it. I want you to remove all my rationalizations and excuses and show me my sin and myself in all their ugliness."

→ That's deep.

Incredibly true! I can relate.

Sometimes we Guilty Souls have such a hard time with being overwhelmed with feelings of guilt that we become afraid to go through the agonies and pain of facing up to our sin. We become at first guilty, then fearful, then discouraged and ultimately, we feel we can never be right with God again. So, although we have felt sorry and even prayed for forgiveness, we feel there is a level of conviction and repentance to which we cannot go. This should not be. To overcome this, we will have to depend on grace. Grace to help us be convicted and grace to forgive us when we are. If we trust in grace to save us, we realize that grace will not only forgive us, but it will teach us what we need to learn about ourselves and our sin in the process. When we can face our sins in this way, we can be truly penitent.

> Cleanse me with hyssop, and I will be clean;
>   wash me, and I will be whiter than snow.
> (Psalm 51:7)

One gets the sense in this verse that David wants to be fully, totally, absolutely forgiven. So forgiven that he feels like new again. All fresh, just like the splendor and cleanliness of freshly fallen snow. If you have never gone out for a walk in newly fallen snow, you have missed a wonderful experience. Nothing is quite so pure, so beautiful. One feels as if the whole world has been made new. It is as if the air, the earth, the whole landscape has been cleansed of every little thing that ever defiled it. Beholding it, you feel you, too, are renewed, refreshed and revived. I have gone out for walks in newly fallen snow and felt so near to God, so absolutely wonderful that it seemed as if a bit of heaven had come down to earth. At moments like these I want the world, and me, to never change, but to remain untainted forever. That is what

David is saying. *God, I want my purity back. I want to be clean again. I want to be fresh, new, pristine, crisp and glorious. Just like the newly fallen, pure white snow. Only you can make it so. Please do so for me.*

> Hide your face from my sins ⟶ *his stain.*
>   and blot out all my iniquity. (Psalm 51:9)

David longs for total forgiveness. He wants God to completely look away from his sins. He wants God to turn his eyes away, not from him, but from his sin. God cannot look upon sin. David has sinned, but he wants God to so remove his sin that when he looks at David, he no longer sees his sin. He wants God's eyes upon him again, but asks that God's eyes not see his sin. He wants all of his iniquity blotted out. Completely, totally gone. He wants it all taken away so that the stain is removed from his soul.

> Let me hear joy and gladness;
>   let the bones you have crushed rejoice....
> Do not cast me from your presence
>   or take your Holy Spirit from me.
> Restore to me the joy of your salvation
>   and grant me a willing spirit, to sustain me.
> (Psalm 51:8,11–12)

David asks for the restoration of his joy. Think about it for a moment, Guilty Soul. Do we not feel we must remain in misery and depression for a time—perhaps the rest of our life—as a way of atoning for our sin? Certainly James teaches us to "grieve, mourn and wail," and there is a time for sorrow and apology to God and to others. But there comes a time when we are to not only be forgiven, but to feel forgiven. And then, not only to feel forgiven, but to be happy again. Not just to be occasionally happy, but to once more possess a sense of the true, deep-down joy of salvation.

David says in effect, "God, I don't want to stay down. I don't want to remain forever in grief and misery. In your grace, not only forgive me, but let be happy again." When we think about it, we could regard this as a presumptuous, selfish request. Remember what he did: he deliberately took advantage of his position of trust and power to commit adultery and murder. And now he asks to be happy again! How can he do this? Not because he has paid for his crimes. Not because his sorrow for his sin is sufficient to earn this privilege. He can ask this solely on the basis of the grace of God.

He longs for intimacy with God again. He begs not to be cast away from God. David is so dependent on grace that he requests for the most precious gifts of fellowship with God and the presence of God's Spirit to remain with him. He asks this not because he is confident of himself, but because he trusts in God's mercy.

In verse 12 David asks for the motivation to keep going. He asks for the restoration of a willing spirit. Is not one of the results of sin a loss of motivation? Is anything more demotivating than guilt and shame? I don't know about you (I take that back—I *do* know about you!), but when I realize I have sinned, it is so very hard to get back the energy and motivation to serve and give again. I feel that I have in some way let God and others down so much that I can never recover. This is one of the most sinister dangers of sin: a loss of motivation, even when we have done all we can to repent. We imagine God sitting there, distant and aloof, saying, "Okay, you sinned. Now, get your heart humble, tender and get yourself fired up again. It's all up to you." To overcome this we must appeal to God for the grace to help us get back on our feet and get going again.

Create in me a pure heart, O God,
   and renew a steadfast spirit within me.
(Psalm 51:10)

David now asks for a pure heart and for a fresh outpouring of motivation. I think this is one of the most encouraging verses in all of God's word. It takes grace to get our heart right. It takes grace to get motivated again. When we have sinned, we feel we can never get back our hearts again. We feel we have lost our innocence, our sincere purity, our child-like closeness to God. We doubt our hearts can ever be clean again, that we could ever feel truly near to our Father again. We wonder if in some way our heart and life have been irretrievably damaged. So David asks for God to create in him a pure heart. This is amazing, when we grasp what he is really asking. He is asking for God to help him get his insides right. Here is the man after the heart of God asking God to help him once again have that heart.

We are so weak and needy that we must depend on grace to get and keep our hearts pure. One of the signs of a good heart is that we know we don't always have one! All we can do is ask, long and pray. We have to come to God as we are and say, "God, I am in a mess. My heart is hard. My heart is defiled. I have sinned so badly, so deliberately that I cannot get my heart pure. Please help me once again have a pure and tender heart."

What else can we do except depend on grace in this way? Even in repenting, we need grace to help us. Ultimately, we are not saved by the degree of brokenness of heart or realization of sin, but by the grace of God. And we need grace to help us get to a place of humility and brokenness.

Then I will teach transgressors your ways,

> and sinners will turn back to you.
> Save me from bloodguilt, O God,
>   the God who saves me,
>   and my tongue will sing of your righteousness.
> O Lord, open my lips,
>   and my mouth will declare your praise.
> (Psalm 51:13–15)

David closes his prayer saying that he intends and longs to once again be a help to others. He declares that he will once again teach transgressors the ways of God. Not only is he to be forgiven by grace, but grace will restore him to a place of usefulness. Sometimes we feel we have so blown it that we can never again be used to help others. What an empty life that would be! It is as if God is saying to us, "You are forgiven, but now you are useless. The best you can hope for is to hang in there and maybe make it to heaven. But you can forget about ever being used by me again. No way." I guess we need to tell that to Abraham, Moses, Elijah, Jonah, Peter, John Mark and just about every Biblical character. Who of them did not fail, and even fail miserably at some point? Is that not part of what draws us to them, that they were "like us" (James 5:17)?

David went on to be used again by God. I am sure he carried the memory of his sins with him to his grave, but he did not fade into obscurity and uselessness. One of the great things about David's life is that he teaches us not only how to be close to God, but how to repent when we have failed him. We have focused on a moment of great failure in David's life, one of the worst lapses recorded of any character in Scripture. The great majority of the sins we commit will not be at this level of intensity or consequence. We do not need to treat everything we do or fail to do as if it were equal to

David's sin in this instance. Sins vary in the level of consequence. All sin is serious, and all sin crucified Jesus, but common sense tells us that not all sin is of equal import or requires the same intensity of response.

Guilty Souls tend to put all sin in the same category and go through a Psalm 51 level of repentance for every sin they commit. This is not necessary and will ultimately lead us to spiritual frustration and defeat. Such an overreaction will wear us out and leave us discouraged in our attempt to live a holy, committed life.

Part of maturity is learning how to react properly to the different mistakes we make. This is where other Christians can help us get a proper sense of perspective and give us a sober, rational judgment of our conduct. (See chapter 25 for a more extensive treatment of this subject.)

Let us learn from David. Let us strive to be tenderhearted in our relationship with our Father. Let us strive to be truthful and open with him. Even when David was blind to his sin, God mercifully sent Nathan to rebuke and awaken him. And, as he strove to repent, David received grace from God not only to be forgiven, but to help him get his heart and mind all the way home. May we believe, as David did, that God's grace is available to us.

Chapter 23

Claiming Grace

Praise the LORD, O my soul;
  all my inmost being, praise his holy name.
Praise the LORD, O my soul,
  and forget not all his benefits—
who forgives all your sins
  and heals all your diseases,
who redeems your life from the pit
  and crowns you with love and compassion,
who satisfies your desires with good things
  so that your youth is renewed like the eagle's.
  Psalm 103:1–5

For many Guilty Souls, grace is the unclaimed prize. It has been given, but never truly received. Oh, we believe in grace in the sense that we know we need it to be saved and that we could never make it to heaven without it. But in another sense, grace remains dormant. It is the unopened gift, the blessing not enjoyed. It is accepted only in theory, but not in practice. It is absent in our emotional life, in the real world in which we live and move and have our being.

How can we get grace into our mind and into our deepest heart?

We have previously looked to David to learn about grace. Now, take another trip with me back into the very soul of the man after God's own heart. Let us look even deeper into the relationship David had with God. But let us do more than that, let us pray his prayers and sing his songs.

Try this. In your next time of private devotion, open your Bible to Psalm 103. Go to a place of prayer, one of the places where you feel inspired, safe and alone with God. While there, pray your way through this great psalm. Let the words of this song of praise become your words.

If you have never prayed the psalms before, it may seem a bit awkward at first. Don't let this stop you. I believe one reason God left us the book of Psalms is to teach us how to worship, pray and praise. Praying the psalms will take you places that study alone will not. It will take you to a place of expressing to God the things that David did. It will take you to a place of emotional intimacy that you might never attain on your own. David had a freedom of expression in his walk with God that we all desperately need. Let yourself go there.

It was at one of the lowest points of my life when I taught myself to pray through this psalm. I felt defeated, discouraged and useless. My life and efforts in the ministry seemed to be in reverse gear. Some dear relatives were struggling spiritually, and deep wounds had been inflicted upon me by some who doubted my motives.

In the midst of this sorrow it dawned upon me that whatever happened, I needed to claim God's love, remember his blessings, rejoice in his mercy and rest in his grace. I had been praying through other psalms, ones in which David poured out his sorrows, confessed his weakness and sin, and cast himself upon God. That was all well and good, but I sensed there was a missing element. I did not see any immediate relief coming in my situation (and indeed, none came for several years). I knew God could work a miracle and suddenly reverse the situation, but I also knew that there was no guarantee or promise that he would do so. I knew that I needed to go to another level of dependency on God, not just for deliverance, but for thanksgiving, appreciation and gratitude. I needed to see and accept grace at a deeper level than I ever had before.

But how could I get there? I decided to pray my way through Psalm 103, remembering as I did all the blessings and grace that it described. David began his prayer by appealing to his soul to praise God. As I did this, I realized that sometimes we have to talk to our own soul. Sometimes we have to tell our soul to do something that it may resist doing. As I prayed I certainly did not feel an overwhelming sense of God's grace. I felt very awkward and unsure, even insincere, because my emotions were at such a low point.

As I prayed through verses 1–5, I remembered that God had forgiven all my sins. He had *forgiven.* My sins were gone; they were in his mind no more. No longer did they stand between us. He had forgiven *all* my sins. Those sins whose selfishness and pain still stung me, he had forgiven. Even more than David, I could have the certitude of forgiveness because of the cleansing blood of Jesus. I remembered that God had *healed* me of the diseases of my life, and I thought of how Jesus the Great Physician had in the past healed me of so many hurts and wounds, resulting from my sins and those committed against me.

I prayed about how he had *redeemed* me from the pits. I prayed through my whole life and recalled the pits I had fallen into. I remembered how God in his grace had always reached down and drawn me out, even when I was close to giving up. I thought of the *crown of dignity and honor* that God had given me, my salvation and high purpose. I thought of how he had given honor to me and how much he loved me, and more than that, how with *compassion* he felt for me and with me in what I was going through. I prayed about how he satisfied my desires to make a meaningful contribution by giving me opportunities to serve him and his people. In spite of the fact that it seemed at that moment that my ministry and efforts were insignificant, they were not so to God. This all made me feel full of life and hope, and renewed me and let me believe I could, like the eagle, soar again.

After I prayed my way through that psalm, the sky was a little brighter, and my soul felt a great deal lighter. I was amazed at how my emotions changed in that hour of prayer. My problems did not all vanish, and I still had to face them, but I did so with greater confidence. And that came, not by analyzing grace, but by claiming it in prayer. I have had to do this many times since then, with other psalms, and with other prayers and other problems. I have prayed the same way using Paul's prayer in Ephesians 1:3–14 and 3:14–21 as well.

This is my story of praying through prayers in the Bible. You need to live out your own story and make your own claim on grace. I urge you to do so. Go to God and claim his grace. Praise him and thank him to the limit you are capable, even if it seems awkward and artificial at first. This is where you must decide to love God with your mind and think the thoughts he wants you to think, no matter what you feel.

This is not the only way to claim grace, but it is a good way. It is a Biblical way. It is a way traveled by the man after the heart of God and countless others who have let his inspired words guide them to a better place. Try it, and don't give up. Claim God's grace in prayer.

Part 3
LIVING IN GRACE

Chapter 24

Grace and Discipline

In your struggle against sin, you have not yet resisted to the point of shedding your blood. And you have forgotten that word of encouragement that addresses you as sons:

> "My son, do not make light of the Lord's discipline,
> and do not lose heart when he rebukes you,
> because the Lord disciplines those he loves,
> and he punishes everyone he accepts as a son."

Endure hardship as discipline; God is treating you as sons. For what son is not disciplined by his father?

Hebrews 12:4–7

To keep me from becoming conceited because of these surpassingly great revelations, there was given me a thorn in my flesh, a messenger of Satan, to torment me. Three times I pleaded with the Lord to take it away from me. But he said to me, "My grace is sufficient for you, for my power is made perfect in weakness." Therefore I will boast all the more gladly about my weaknesses, so that Christ's power may rest on me. That is why, for Christ's sake, I delight in weaknesses, in insults, in hardships, in persecutions, in difficulties. For when I am weak, then I am strong.

2 Corinthians 12:7–10

Discipline is a fact of life for Christians. God puts each of us through our paces. When we sign up to follow him, we

very true

115

enter into a life of being disciplined by our heavenly Father.
That all seems well and good, but for the Guilty Soul, God's
discipline can be another source of condemnation, because
the Guilty Soul often equates God's discipline with his displeasure or disapproval.

Could this view be accurate? Does God ever directly punish us for our sin? Yes, it could be, and yes, he does. God
sometimes directly deals with sin, as in the case of David.
When David committed adultery and murder and lied to
cover it up, he suffered. God was upset with David. God let
his child die, and he let David suffer the consequences of his
actions. As Nathan said, "Now, therefore, the sword will
never depart from your house, because you despised me and
took the wife of Uriah the Hittite to be your own" (2 Samuel
12:10).

But we must remember that David suffered at other times
when there was no sin on his part. For example, David suffered terribly when he was driven away by Saul and had to
live alone as a fugitive in the desert. His banishment was not
God's punishment for sin. He suffered because of the sins of
another. And in the midst of the trial, God used it for his
greater sovereign purpose and also for the special purpose of
disciplining and training David.

This was the same type of thing Joseph went through
when his brothers sold him into slavery. As with David's suffering, this was not an occasion of God's punishment. His suffering was a part of a greater plan, a plan for "the saving of
many lives" (Genesis 50:20) that God worked out over the
course of many years.

Paul was not being punished when he was given the thorn
in the flesh. He was being disciplined. He was not given the

thorn because God was angry with him or even disappointed in him. He was given the thorn to keep him humble and to make him dependent on grace. Paul still had a strong will, you see, and he had a tendency to pride. And although God knew this about Paul, it did not make him angry; instead it awakened his Fatherly care.

So in his love and wisdom, God gave Paul a weakness, a weakness that humbled and even embarrassed Paul. We don't know what it was, but we do know that Paul asked three times for it to be taken away. And we remember God's answer: No. This was not a punishment for Paul's past sins, nor was it a punishment for the besetting sin of pride. It was not punishment, but discipline. It was not a sign of anger or disgust, or even of displeasure. It was instead the sign of a loving Father helping his dear son with a well-known fault.

Paul looked at his thorn in the flesh that way. He knew that behind it lurked his old nemesis, pride. He knew that pride was the sin that had made him the self-righteous persecutor he had been. He knew that pride still crouched at his door and was ever near him, always ready to take him down. But Paul was also aware that God was not displeased with him because of his continued struggles. This realization caused Paul to feel loved and cared for rather than guilty and rejected.

He knew his thorn in the flesh was a gift of grace, motivated by love, not by anger or displeasure. And so he embraced the thorn as the discipline of a kind, gracious and loving Father, not of an angry, vengeful and distant taskmaster. He was assured that God, although seeing his sinful tendency, still loved and liked him. He knew that in spite of this God wanted to use him.

Let me ask a few questions:

Why do we have to see displeasure in every discipline and punishment in every trial? When will we learn to embrace our disciplines, not as a sign of distance but of devotion from our heavenly Father?

Will we see that hardships in our lives are not necessarily God's punishments but his gracious disciplines? Can we realize that although God sees our besetting sins more clearly than we do, he still loves and likes us, desires fellowship with us, and wants to help us overcome them? Can we see that some sins will always tempt us, that without our careful watchfulness, we could fall back? And can we see that such a reality is not unexpected, that God knew it would be this way and planned for a life-long process of discipline to help us grow?

Last year we made a move, leaving behind many dear friends and a congregation we loved with all of our hearts. My mother passed away during the summer. During this time we also underwent a time of criticism, turmoil and soul-searching, and many of our friends were struggling spiritually. And then, in the midst of this difficult and stressful year, Geri began noticing persistent, increasing numbness in her body. After many tests, she was diagnosed with Multiple Sclerosis.

We were tempted to wonder what we had done to so displease God that would cause him to do all of this to us. But we studied our Bibles, prayed and realized that God's love and grace were unfailing, and that whatever we were going through was meant to make us more like Christ and to make us better people.

We decided to trust in God's love and to seek to learn all we could from the trials we were experiencing. We are still learning, and God is still teaching. We feel closer to God and more dependent on him than at any time in our lives. And during all of this, our Father in heaven has never stopped pouring out upon us his countless blessings.

Will we trust in God's grace? Will we join our spiritual forebears in the Band of the Beloved Disciplined? Let us join them, knowing that the hardships we face are not the punishments of an angry God, but the gracious disciplines of a loving Father.

Chapter 25

When the Guilty Soul
Really Is Guilty

There is not a righteous man on earth
who does what is right and never sins.
Ecclesiastes 7:20

If we claim to be without sin, we deceive ourselves and the truth is not in us. If we confess our
sins, he is faithful and just and will forgive us our sins
and purify us from all unrighteousness. If we claim we
have not sinned, we make him out to be a liar and his
word has no place in our lives.

My dear children, I write this to you so that you
will not sin. But if anybody does sin, we have one who
speaks to the Father in our defense—Jesus Christ, the
Righteous One. He is the atoning sacrifice for our sins,
and not only for ours but also for the sins of the whole
world.

1 John 1:8–2:2

Therefore confess your sins to each other and pray for
each other so that you may be healed. The prayer of a
righteous man is powerful and effective.

James 5:16

Guilty Souls are sinners, too. Having an overactive

conscience does not mean that we are immune to sin. Guilty Souls are not only capable of sin, but we do sin, and we sin just like everyone else. It's just that we Guilty Souls tend to make it more complicated when we sin, as we do in most areas of life.

The Bible does not promise us that we will never sin again after we become Christians. It does say we are forgiven and that we have the Holy Spirit to help us overcome our sin and that God will not let us be put in a situation where sin is inevitable.

> No temptation has seized you except what is common to man. And God is faithful; he will not let you be tempted beyond what you can bear. But when you are tempted, he will also provide a way out so that you can stand up under it. (1 Corinthians 10:13)

But this promise does not change the reality that even the most sincere, purehearted Christian will sin. Otherwise, why would we be taught how to deal with sin after we are Christians? If even great heroes like Peter can sin after years of walking with the Lord, what about the rest of us?

Some Guilty Souls react so strongly to their sin and with such intense self-criticism, that they actually impede the process of repentance. It does not help us to overcome sin if we cast ourselves into one of the outer rings of hell over every stumbling. Far better to see our sin in proper proportion and go on from there.

Be Sorry for Your Sin

> Submit yourselves, then, to God. Resist the devil, and he will flee from you. Come near to God and he will come near to you. Wash your hands, you sinners, and purify your hearts, you double-minded. Grieve, mourn and wail. Change your laughter to mourning and your

joy to gloom. <u>Humble yourselves before the Lord</u>, <u>and</u>
<u>he will lift you up.</u> (James 4:7–10)

When we sin, it should sadden us. It should disappoint us.
It should cause us to mourn. We cannot mumble, "Excuse
me, Lord" and blithely go on our way. Nor can we take sin
lightly as if it were not that serious a thing. To do so is to
diminish God's holiness and presume upon his grace. It is the
gravity of sin that makes grace so amazing.

How sorry do we have to be? Here is where it gets tricky
for the Guilty Soul. We have to learn *a sense of proportion* in
dealing with our sin. All sin is sin, and all sin is wrong. But not
all sin is equal in its results. Being abrupt or rude to someone
is not on the same level as deeply resenting, hating, cursing or
physically attacking them.

Let your sorrow be proportional to the degree of harm your
sin has caused to your relationship to God or to another person.
If you have been rude or thoughtless to a friend, seek to understand how they felt as a result of your actions. Let your focus
be upon what is right and how *they* feel rather than how *you*
feel. Be sorrowful and tell them so. If you have slighted someone, that is one thing, but if you have deeply harmed them,
then your sorrow needs to intensify.

This does not mean you are always responsible for all that
another may feel. There may have been a genuine misunderstanding, or the other person may have assumed there were
motives and intentions you did not have. Perhaps they have
overreacted due to issues within themselves. You need to listen and carefully evaluate what you hear. Human relationships can get complicated, and we must strive for perspective.

Even if I caused you sorrow by my letter, I do not
regret it. Though I did regret it—I see that my letter

hurt you, but only for a little while—yet now I am happy, not because you were made sorry, but because your sorrow led you to repentance. For you became sorrowful as God intended and so were not harmed in any way by us. Godly sorrow brings repentance that leads to salvation and leaves no regret, but worldly sorrow brings death. See what this godly sorrow has produced in you: what earnestness, what eagerness to clear yourselves, what indignation, what alarm, what longing, what concern, what readiness to see justice done. At every point you have proved yourselves to be innocent in this matter. (2 Corinthians 7:8–11)

As we talked about in the chapter on "Godly Sorrow, Worldly Sorrow," godly sorrow brings repentance. When we see we have hurt God or another person, we should be sorry. How sorry? Sorry enough to admit our wrong and to be moved to repent. Our responsibility is to see our sin, grieve over it, and change. We must guard against being hardhearted or numb to our sin.

It is often difficult to quantify how much sorrow we should feel over our sin. Can any of us ever feel enough sorrow? Will we ever know the pain we caused Jesus or our Father in heaven? Will we ever fully understand how much we have grieved another person? I am not saying we should not try. I am not saying we should not seek to see our sin. But I am saying that even with our best efforts, we sometimes can only get so far in the amount of sorrow we can feel or express. Forgiveness and grace are not conditioned upon the degree of perfection we attain in coming to a particular emotional state. A closer look at Paul's description of the characteristics of godly sorrow in 2 Corinthians 7:11 can help us: *earnestness, eagerness to clear yourselves, indignation, alarm, longing, concern, readiness to see justice done.* The focus here seems to be upon a willingness to see any wrong and an eagerness to see the right thing done. The Corinthians listened, changed and took action—with heartfelt sincerity.

We do ourselves and our relationship to God no good when we cast ourselves into bondage in striving to attain an imagined perfect degree of sorrow for sin. We do well to pray, fast, study, listen and open our hearts to conviction. But we also need to give God time to teach us all we need to see as we seek deeper sensitivity to our sins. Even in coming to the proper level of conviction of sin, we need grace to help us. After his rebuke from Nathan, did David immediately and fully see all the pain his sin caused God or others? Whatever he understood initially, he certainly realized more as he saw the consequences of his sin in the lives of his children. In Psalm 51 David longs to see his sin and prays for his heart to be enlightened, but he leaves room for God to teach him these lessons in the future.

The longer I live as a Christian, the more I see the depth of my sin and my selfishness. Both in a general sense and in seeing specific things I have done, my conscience has been awakened as I have walked with God through the years. How many times has a painful memory come back to convict me as I have prayed or read my Bible! How often I have winced as I have heard my own words or those of others and made a connection with some situation I remember from years past! I believe the Spirit works at these moments to bring us to a deeper, more mature and godly understanding of ourselves and our sin. At those times I remember and I am humbled, but I am also thankful that God is still working to bring enlightenment to the eyes of my heart.

We need to learn this lesson not only in dealing with

ourselves but with others as well. We must avoid holding hostage those who have hurt us until they fully "get it." We do this when we adopt the attitude: "I will not forgive you until you see it just like I think you should. You need to 'get it' before I forgive you. You need to clearly and accurately understand my pain first." If we do this, we are forgetting that we too are sinners and that God does not treat us this way. We must give others room to grow and the opportunity to let God teach them. We must strive to be as gracious to others as God has been to us.

Confess Your Sin

Confession means agreeing with God. It means "to admit, to say plainly." It is that simple. When you sin, agree with God about it. Say it plainly. Call it what it is. Use Biblical terminology to identify your sin. If you lusted, admit it and say it. If you gossiped, say it. If you harbored hatred, resentment or bitterness, say it. Make no excuses. Make no rationalizations. Don't blame anyone else. Take responsibility.

Here again, we Guilty Souls sometimes do ourselves in when we deal with our sin. Because we think we must become painfully miserable when we admit sin, we may tend to avoid dealing with it altogether. We simply choose not to go there. Far better to plainly confess and deal with sin before God and go on. If we make repentance an ordeal of penance rather than a process of honest confession, we hamper our ability to overcome our sin. Grace means that when we sin, we can confess and be forgiven. If you are the kind of Guilty Soul that inflicts punishment upon yourself, you can ultimately end up avoiding dealing with your sin to escape self-punishment.

Repent of Sin

[Repentance] is a change of mind and will that leads to a change in behavior. It is not based on emotion. "But how do I know if I have really repented?" asks the Guilty Soul. Don't make it more complicated than it is! Make a decision to repent, pray about it, and go on. This is the usual way to deal with sin as we go through our day. If you are struggling with a persistent sin or a more serious transgression, you may need to take stronger measures. There are some practical ways to reinforce your decision and come to closure. Perhaps you need to write a letter to God. A helpful Biblical solution is to confess to a friend and ask him or her to pray for you and to help you:

> He who conceals his sins does not prosper,
>> but whoever confesses and renounces them
>>> finds mercy. (Proverbs 28:13)

Therefore confess your sins to each other and pray for each other so that you may be healed. The prayer of a righteous man is powerful and effective. (James 5:16)

Accept Forgiveness

With God, dealing with sin is a straightforward thing. He wants us to see it, be sorry for it, confess and repent. We are then forgiven. We can then go on with our life.

Jesus often said, "Your sins are forgiven. Go in peace." This sense of closure needs to come to our hearts and minds as we deal with sin. It is not that we lightly dismiss our sin or that we are not humbled by it. Like David, we should say, "For I know my transgressions, and my sin is always before me" (Psalm 51:3). Like Paul, who said he was the worst of sinners (1 Timothy 1:15), we should never forget who we were or what we did. Nor should we forget who we would become if not for the continued work of grace. But there is a difference in having a healthy remembrance of our past transgressions and in never fully accepting God's pardon.

Some of us, if we were the prodigal son, would spurn our father's forgiveness and insist on banishment to the servant's quarters. We would deny our father a restored relationship with us and would break his heart in the process. We would not only cheat ourselves out of grace, but would deny the other members of the household a great party!

As long as we are in this life, we will have to deal with sin. We will grow and change, but we will never attain a sin-free existence. And when we sin, may we turn to God and claim the grace that he has made continually available through Christ.

Chapter 26

Grace and Adversity

It was good for me to be afflicted
so that I might learn your decrees.

Psalm 119:71

This morning the tranquility of my writing vacation was interrupted by news of adversity. Our church is purchasing a ten-acre tract on a main thoroughfare, and we are in the process of getting approval to build. One of the county commissioners is a notorious opponent of just about any building project, and he has gone into the adjacent neighborhood and stirred up opposition against the project. The meeting happened last night, and we hastily rallied about thirty of our members to attend and represent our case as best they could. The vote was tabled, and we now have our work cut out for us to reassure the residents that we will be good neighbors, that their fears and suspicions are unfounded, and that a church is a far better alternative to other projects that could end up on that tract.

My thoughts and reactions are instructive for a Guilty Soul:

What did I do wrong?
I knew the meeting was coming; why didn't I anticipate this?

I have not provided the wise, visionary leadership the church has needed.

I don't like conflict. I don't want to get into this.

See, this proves you are not a good leader. A leader has no fear, never flinches, but leads the troops forward into battle. You are no good.

Is God going to answer our prayers?

Do we have enough faith?

How will the congregation respond?

On and on I could go. I suppose this is part confession, part me working this out.

How do you react when adversity comes your way? What are your instinctive thoughts? The Guilty Soul generally has several.

'This is all my fault.'

If we blame all our adversities on our sins and weaknesses, we are not only unwise, but we are also not depending on grace. Sometimes sin is the *root* of an adversity; sometimes it is a *response* to an adversity; sometimes it is a *part* of the problem, and sometimes it has *nothing to do* with the problem. Guilty Souls will often search for our own sin as the primary cause of any adversity. We will dig through the files of memory and history to come up with the juncture where, if we had had more faith, more foresight, more courage, more wisdom, we could have prevented the adversity from ever having happened.

Guilty Souls are their own critic, accuser and enemy. Unlike Job, they would join with their well-meaning but misguided friends and look for some personal fault upon which to blame the miseries that beset them. In answer to Paul's question in

Romans 8, "Who is there to condemn?" Guilty Souls have no
further to look than in the mirror. "Me! I condemn me!" is their
cry. Satan doesn't even have to help; we do his job for him. I
suppose that leaves the devil free to go work on somebody else,
since we are carrying out what he normally would have to do for
himself.

'God must be displeased with me, or this would not have happened.'

We equate God's approval with everything going well,
flowing smoothly and working out without glitches, struggles,
conflict or setbacks. Even a cursory reading of the Bible
shows this to be faulty thinking.

Sometimes sin is the reason we have setbacks. Check out
the defeats of the children of Israel caused by their lack of
faith in Numbers 13 and 14:39–45. Take a look at what happened at Ai in Joshua 7 and to Ananias and Sapphira in Acts 5.

But look carefully before blaming God's displeasure for
every adversity encountered by his people. Was God passing
judgment on Joseph's sin when he was sold into Egyptian
slavery by his brothers? Was Elijah out of favor with God
when Jezebel threatened to kill him after his victory over the
false prophets on Mount Carmel? Were Nehemiah and the
residents of Jerusalem under divine disapproval when their
enemies initiated a slander campaign against them as they
attempted to rebuild the walls of the city? Was it because of
God's dissatisfaction with Paul that some jealous preachers
stepped up their efforts to discredit the apostle when he was
in a Roman prison?

Adversity can be caused by God's opposition due to our
sin. But it can also come from the fact that someone else, be
it Satan himself or some misguided person, is against us and

the good we are trying to do. So think carefully before plunging into the abyss of guilt the next time you face a trial. External adversity is difficult enough without you becoming your own internal accuser.

'This happened because of sin in my life.'

Adversity often reveals or provokes a sinful attitude or response in us. Peter in anger drew a sword and cut off the ear of the servant of the high priest during the arrest of Jesus. James and John asked for fire from heaven to incinerate the Samaritan innkeeper who denied them lodging. Moses got angry and struck the rock when he had finally had enough of the grumblers and gripers. These are all examples of sin, to be sure, (and numerous other examples from the Scriptures could be cited), but none of these sinful responses indicate that the adversity was caused by sin. The adversity exposed weakness, it did not create it. The adversity was not sent by God as a punishment. And although God disciplined and corrected the sins of those involved in some way, he did not utterly reject them or disqualify them as his servants. Even for the sin of denying Christ, Peter was graciously given forgiveness, restoration of his relationship with Jesus and a role of leadership in the early church.

God meets our adversities with grace, and the more we understand this, the better we will be at facing and overcoming them.

Adversity can come from sin, and God may be opposing us, but carefully check out the facts before assuming sin is to blame. Before automatically invoking "God opposes the proud, but gives grace to the humble" (James 4:6; 1 Peter 5:5), consider that there may be another plan at work. And remember, there has to be adversity to overcome in the first place before it is necessary for God to give grace to the humble!

Part of being humble is realizing we need grace to face the adversity that has come upon us. If we turn to God for grace when adversity confronts us, then we are responding with faith and humility. If we always assume God is against us, we are not trusting him. We short-circuit the learning process and are cast upon our own devices.

Remember, grace means depending on God's good attitude towards us, not just upon his ability to help us. For the Guilty Soul, more than half the battle is believing that in setbacks and difficulties God is with us, and will still be with us even when we show a lack of faith or respond with selfishness, anger or pride in the face of adversity.

Don't bail out of believing God is with you when adversity comes. Even when your response is not initially what it should be, you can by grace recover. How about the disciples in the boat that day when the storm came (Mark 4:35–41)? They panicked in fear, they doubted, they even questioned whether or not Jesus cared. "Teacher, don't you care if we drown?" was their cry. Jesus corrected them, but he did not give up on them. He went ahead and stilled the waves.

How many other times do we see Jesus make a similar response to an improper reaction in the face of adversity? How about his handling of the father of the epileptic boy (Mark 9:14–29)? This man lacked faith and admitted it. "If you can do anything," he said, "take pity on us and help us." But even in the face of his weak faith, Jesus graciously healed his son.

Too often we think that until we have perfect faith, God will not help us. The Bible teaches and demonstrates otherwise. On many occasions in the Scriptures adversity was met with a faith that was anything but flawless. Our faith is not just in the ability of God, but in the graciousness and good- ness of God. Our faith is in a God who "remembers that we are dust" (Psalm 103:14), who knows that we act like children at times and that we are only too human. *Our faith is not in the greatness of our own faith, but in the faithfulness of God. We must be more consumed with the ability and willingness of God to help us than with our own level of trust.* ➔ I agree.

I am not saying that doubt is good or that we do not need to grow in faith. I am saying that God does not abandon us if our faith falters and that he can and will use those moments as opportunities to help our faith to grow.

If we walk away from God and forsake him, then that is a very serious matter. But tell me, would we not be more likely to do that if we believed God were intractably angry with us, that he did not care about us, and that he had no mercy upon us in the face of our weaknesses?

So then, in the face of adversity, do not automatically assume your sin is the root of the adversity. Be willing to see any sin, but do not go into a tailspin of guilt.

Do not think that because you do not respond as you should to adversity, that God will abandon you until you completely, perfectly change.

Do not think that your sinful response during adversity meant that God was angry with you all along and just couldn't wait to let you know.

Do not think you must have perfect faith, or the faith of some stronger Christian, for God to hear your prayers.

Do not think that even faith mixed with fear and doubt

won't get some great results.

Do not think that until you totally understand all you need to learn from the adversity, God is unhappy and distant from you.

(Oh, by the way. I feel much better about the building project after writing all this out. Now that I think about it, I'm not such a bad leader after all. The church will come out fine. God will use this to build the faith of our congregation. If the project gets torpedoed, he has something better for us anyway. I really do feel better now. Thanks for listening. I think I'll hit the "save" button and have some lunch.)

Chapter 27

Grace in the Hour of Need

Let us then approach the throne of grace with confidence, so that we may receive mercy and find grace to help us in our time of need.

●Hebrews 4:16

All the grace you ever needed was not used up on the day of your salvation. It will be needed throughout your life—over and over again.

You will need it when you sin and once again need forgiveness.

You will need it when you fail and once again need strength and encouragement.

You will need it when you lack wisdom in the face of thorny, seemingly insoluble problems.

You will need it when temptation looks too good and too strong to resist.

You will need it when granting forgiveness to another seems impossible.

You will need it when your motivation and desire to serve God is almost gone.

Grace is more than a principle; it is a source of immediate strength and help. It is available to us all the time, 24/7. It is available, and it is needed. Not that we need to be saved all over again, but that we need it for deliverance from specific sins in specific moments and in specific situations.

The problem is that in the hour of need we may not feel particularly worthy or righteous. Why else would we be needy if that were not the case? Unless we are weak, assaulted by temptation or doubt, we do not feel keenly the need for help. But it is then that Guilty Souls can do themselves in. We can reason this way: "Here I am again, weak, failing, doubting. Here I am again, in need. *Here I am again.* I ought to be stronger than this. I ought to have more faith than this. I should have never let myself get in this situation. God must be so upset with me. I can't even pray about this."

Do you see where this is going? Ever gone there? I have, many times. It is as if we are saying we have no right to ask for grace when we have once again proven we need it. It is as if we think grace was given to us to forgive us when we became Christians, but once that is past, we are on our own. No more excuses! No more grace! Any more failures and weakness will not be tolerated! Your account is empty, all used up, no more mercy!

I don't know about you, but sometimes when I am tempted to sin, or have sinned, I feel so tainted, so dirty and selfish, so disappointed in myself that I just want to avoid talking to God. I am too ashamed to come to him and say, "Here I am again. Yea, me. Same old guy. Same old struggles. Same old sin. Same old needs." When we sin, and our conscience is defiled, there is a sense of feeling unclean before God, of feeling stained and soiled. I don't like coming to God at those times or when I am

I think the same thoughts

in the throes of temptation. If I have lusted or been angry, if I have had bitter thoughts about someone, it is hard for me to come before God in the midst of the struggle.

Yet I must come to God in the midst of it. I need grace at that moment. At the moment of weakness, when I am genuinely being drawn into sin, at that moment I need the grace of God. No matter how weak and dirty I feel, no matter how alluring sin is, at that moment I must go to the throne of grace with boldness and confidence, and admitting my situation, appeal to God to send forth his grace in my life. Grace to help me get my thinking right. Grace to help me deal with the pull of sin. Grace to cleanse away the dirt that sin has smeared upon me. Grace to help me walk away from my most selfish, evil desires. Grace that sees me at my worse, with my most evil, selfish thoughts and reflections, but that lifts me up out of all that into a better place.

It takes a real trust in grace to come before the throne of God at moments of failure or weakness. But we can be encouraged because that is just what Jesus did. When he prayed in the Garden, saying, "Not my will, but yours be done," he recognized the need to surrender his will. He was tempted to put his own desires above God's will and above our needs. He took his honest desires before God, and while admitting them, surrendered them. He did not allow the fact that he was being tempted discourage him or take him away from his Father, but to draw him nearer.

This is what we must remember: when we are tempted, when we are at our weakest, most embarrassing moments of selfishness and failure, we must come to God for grace. We must come freely. Quickly. Boldly. Repeatedly. There, at his righteous throne, a fresh supply of grace awaits us. Grace to help us in our hour of need.

Chapter 28

Grace and Pride

"Every valley shall be raised up,
    every mountain and hill made low;
the rough ground shall become level,
    the rugged places a plain.
And the glory of the LORD will be revealed,
    and all mankind together will see it.
For the mouth of the LORD has spoken."

Isaiah 40:4–5

Only God knows how to humble us and exalt us at the same time. Only he knows how to humble our pride and yet build up our confidence. Only he knows how to raise us up from the valley of self-criticism and bring down our mountains of arrogance. There is no one else to whom we can turn to make this happen, no one but God himself can do this for us.

Grace is a reminder that we can never be good enough on our own. It tells us that our best efforts fall miserably short and that we cannot bootstrap our way up to the Lord. Is that humbling? You better believe it. We can't earn it. We can't be good enough. We are too sinful, and God is too holy.

Pride is a terrible sin. It is the greatest sin because it utterly destroys our relationship with God. God made us to live in dependence on him. Pride says that we are self-sustaining and that we do not need God's help or his forgiveness.

One way for our pride to be broken is by seeing our sin. We must come face to face with how ugly, selfish and destructive our sin is. Like Peter, when we see the Lord and we see our sin and we remember his word, we go out and weep bitterly (Luke 22:62). Like David, we sometimes have to have a Nathan come and say to us, "You are the man" (2 Samuel 12:7). We need to see our guilt before a holy God, and we need to tremble at his word.

But there is another way for our pride to be broken and for our hearts to be humbled: by encountering God's grace. Our hearts can be softened by seeing how much we are loved and cared for, and how deeply God feels for us. Rather than making us arrogant and unappreciative, this amazing love can work its way into the crevices of our hardened heart and soften it. We can be melted by love, not just broken by sin.

Do you think the prodigal son was made arrogant or humble by his father's gracious forgiveness? He asked his father to allow him to live with the servants, and yet he was treated like a prince. What do you think was the result?

Do you think Peter was made prideful by Jesus' gracious reinstatement in John 21? You don't have to look too far to see that Peter lived the rest of his life in humble service to Jesus in response to the grace that he received.

What about Paul? He deserved condemnation, but he received grace and mercy. What did this do for him? It made him more compassionate, more grateful, more humble. God does not treat us as our sins deserve. This humbles our hearts and causes them to melt in loving appreciation.

We all know people who take God's grace for granted.

Most Guilty Souls are determined not to be in that category, so much so that they won't let themselves enjoy God's grace. But cheap grace is not your problem. Your problem is that you are trying to break your pride and soften your heart with only one tool: the hammer of guilt. It is not that this tool is not needed and that the judgment and righteousness of God are never to be brought to bear upon our souls. Far from it. But we also need to hear the message of grace. We need to know the depth of love in our Father's heart. We need to see the love of Jesus and know that his great love can also do the work of humbling us.

Only God knows how to bring down our mountains of pride. He does this not only with his judgment, but with his unmerited love. Listen to the message of grace. Let God's love speak to the depths of your heart. Consider the tender mercies that have been given to you. Let the grace of God do its great work of bringing you down, and lifting you up.

Chapter 29

Grace and Worry

"So do not worry, saying, 'What shall we eat?' or 'What shall we drink?' or 'What shall we wear?' For the pagans run after all these things, and your heavenly Father knows that you need them. But seek first his kingdom and his righteousness, and all these things will be given to you as well. Therefore do not worry about tomorrow, for tomorrow will worry about itself. Each day has enough trouble of its own."

Matthew 6:31–34

He who did not spare his own Son, but gave him up for us all—how will he not also, along with him, graciously give us all things?

Romans 8:32

Worry is doubt that grace will be given in the future. When we worry, we are concluding that God, who took care of our past sins, mistakes and needs, either cannot or will not take care of them in our future. The Guilty Soul's struggle to accept grace not only reaches backward, it reaches forward as well.

When we realize that worry is a failure to believe in and accept grace, it changes the landscape. Now we can deal with worry as a spiritual problem, rather than as a mere psychological issue.

Paul addresses this problem in Romans 5:6–11:

> You see, at just the right time, when we were still powerless, Christ died for the ungodly. Very rarely will anyone die for a righteous man, though for a good man someone might possibly dare to die. But God demonstrates his own love for us in this: While we were still sinners, Christ died for us.
>
> Since we have now been justified by his blood, how much more shall we be saved from God's wrath through him! For if, when we were God's enemies, we were reconciled to him through the death of his Son, how much more, having been reconciled, shall we be saved through his life! Not only is this so, but we also rejoice in God through our Lord Jesus Christ, through whom we have now received reconciliation.

Here Paul states the case that God's grace, given to us before we were saved, guarantees and assures us of his grace in the future. He describes our past life in the most unflattering of terms. He points out that we were *powerless* and *ungodly*, that we were *sinners* and *enemies*. He says that while we were in this terrible condition, Christ died for us, securing our redemption. But then he moves to his logical and wonderful conclusion, reinforcing it with the powerful, twice-repeated phrase *how much more*: "since we have been saved by his blood, *how much more* shall we be saved from God's wrath through him" (v9, emphasis mine). "*How much more*, having been reconciled, shall we be saved through his life!" (v10, emphasis mine).

Do you see it? The giving of grace in the past, when we were completely estranged from God, was amazing. It was proven by the death of Christ. But grace does not end there. That was only the beginning! As wonderful as was the love Christ showed us in dying for our sins, it was only a foretaste of what is to come. God has so much more to give. He will meet our every need. There is *nothing* that can come our way that God cannot and will not help us overcome. Christ now lives in us through his Spirit (Romans 8: 9–11). Our future is secured, purchased by the death of Christ and empowered by his life lived in us.

Paul's logic is airtight. He first reminds us that God went to the trouble to send Jesus to die for us when were sinners— before we cared for him, deeply believed in him or followed him. In view of that, he reasons, *how much more* will God take care of us now that we believe and are trying to serve him? If God was gracious in the past, when we were estranged from him, then surely he will be gracious in the future, now that we belong to him.

Paul concludes this magnificent argument by saying the only thing left for us to do is...rejoice: "Not only is this so, but we also rejoice in God through our Lord Jesus Christ..." (v11). We do more than just hang in there—we rejoice about our future prospects. Far from worrying, we are to live life confidently, exuberantly, boldly, gladly.[1]

But Paul is not finished yet. He makes his case again in Romans 8:31–32 when he says,

> What, then, shall we say in response to this? If God is for us, who can be against us? He who did not spare his own Son, but gave him up for us all—how will he not also, along with him, graciously give us all things?

It is as if Paul knows that we Guilty Souls are stubborn and slow to believe. We may be miserable in our worries, but at least they are familiar miseries! We just don't want to believe God loves us this much. We reason that perhaps God

---

[1] In the NIV translation of Romans 5:9, "rejoice" does not fully convey the sheer exuberance of Paul's language. A better translation could be "exult" (NAS) or "boast" (NRS).

may be weary of helping. It could be that he is out of patience. Maybe we have disappointed him too many times. Perhaps he has lost interest, and although he has helped us in the past, he is now no longer intimately involved in our lives.

May we just call this what it is? *Illogical. Nonsensical. Foolish.*

We need to get a grip here and use our heads. We need to hear what God is saying and believe in his grace for the future as for our past. God has too much invested in us to quit on us now. He is not about to give up on us after proving beyond any doubt that he deeply cares for us and is concerned about our every need.

Read Matthew 6:25–34 and underline every verb in the future tense. Do the same with Hebrews 13:5–6 and any other scripture you can find that deals with God's promises for guidance, help and provision in your future.

Anxiety is a debilitating habit of thought that can only be broken by consciously depending on grace. When we are beset with anxiety, we are not accepting grace. Anxiety is a weakness that is best addressed by claiming the love and grace of God that he promises us for our future.

Believe in God's grace for your future. Count on it, rejoice in it, exult in it. The grace that initially saved you has not run out and never will. It is saving you now and it will save you in the end. The grace that forgave your sin will meet your every need. Jesus, who died for you, now lives in you. Cast away your anxious thoughts, not on the basis of wishful thinking, hyped-up philosophy or a psychological short cut, but on the basis of the unfailing grace of God, which is yours now...and forever.

Chapter 30

Grace and Regret

...and the ransomed of the LORD will return.
They will enter Zion with singing;
    everlasting joy will crown their heads.
Gladness and joy will overtake them,
    and sorrow and sighing will flee away.

                    Isaiah 35:10

Be glad, O people of Zion,
    rejoice in the LORD your God,
for he has given you
    the autumn rains in righteousness.
He sends you abundant showers,
    both autumn and spring rains, as before.
The threshing floors will be filled with grain;
    the vats will overflow with new wine and oil.

"I will repay you for the years the locusts have eaten—
    the great locust and the young locust,
    the other locusts and the locust swarm—
my great army that I sent among you.
You will have plenty to eat, until you are full,
    and you will praise the name of the LORD your
        God,
    who has worked wonders for you;
never again will my people be shamed."

                    Joel 2:23–26

There are some things that cannot be undone. We cannot go back and undo what we did or failed to do. Everyone has regrets. The Guilty Soul has far more than most other people. We can believe we are forgiven and still have regrets. We can feel that God has removed our sin and still experience the pain of what might have been.

Regret can ruin our lives. Regret can take away the joy of today and darken the horizon of tomorrow. Regret can lurk around us like a cloud, forever casting it shadows upon us.

It leaves us with a vague sense of hollowness, of lost opportunity, of damage done that can never be fully mended. Regret can be a painful memory that arises to stain and drain the most joyful days of our lives.

There is the "I wonder what I should have done" kind of regret. Perhaps we were in a situation where we were not sure of the Lord's path for us, when every option open to us seemed to have a dark side all its own. Those moments come into every life. There are times when we are not sure what to do. *Should I make a stand here? Is this worth me speaking up? Would it be meddling and judgmental to express my reservations; would that mean I am a doubter, a non-supporter? Who am I to speak up? Maybe my feelings are rooted in pride and a too-high opinion of myself. If I make this decision, some people will be hurt or disappointed. But if I make another decision, other people will be hurt or disappointed. And God has not told me exactly what to do.*

Regret can come with hindsight. Later, we see things clearly. *I should have seen that coming,* we think. *I should have not been so naive, so foolish, so trusting. If I had had more vision, I could have seen what needed to be done.* Regret assumes a great deal. It assumes we ought to have been more godly than we were. It assumes we should have been omniscient, seeing everything the way God does. It assumes we should have been omnipotent and that our strength and faith were further along than they may have been.

Regret assumes we should have been more like Jesus, or even just like Jesus. "But isn't that our standard?" you ask. Yes, he is our standard, but last time I checked, none of us has gotten to where he is yet. None of us have the moral judgment and clarity that comes from the sinless walk with God that Jesus had.

To overcome regret, we need to see that God in his grace understands that we are not yet perfect, that we have a long way to go, and that we are still immature. We have to understand that God sees us from a Father's perspective, and

> As a father has compassion on his children,
>   so the LORD has compassion on those who fear
>   him;
> for he knows how we are formed,
>   he remembers that we are dust.
> (Psalm 103:13–14)

What about regret from those things we did wrong that we knew were wrong? We may have definitely known better and still failed to do the right thing. We may have gone against God's word, our own conscience, and the godly advice of friends. What about mistakes like those?

We must depend upon God's grace to forgive us and to work things out for good. The Scriptures are replete with examples to help us. What about Peter denying Jesus? He was warned that he would do it, yet he did it anyway. Later in life, in a desire to please people, he compromised again, this time giving in to pressure from the judaizing teachers. He almost led the whole church astray.

Imagine what would have happened had the churches

followed his lead. They would have drifted from the Gospel and gone back into "works" salvation. Only Paul, a man many years his spiritual junior, saved the day. I wonder if after Paul's stinging rebuke, Peter hung his head, saying, "I thought I had gone beyond my compromising days. I am still as weak as on that night in the courtyard of the high priest." Yet, the Scriptures do not tell us of Peter's spiritual demise because it did not occur. God's grace was once again extended to our dear, very human, brother.

What about Abraham, who twice attempted to save his own life by claiming his wife, Sarah, was merely his sister (Genesis 12:10–20, 20:1–13)? What about Jacob, who deceived and cheated his brother Esau out of his birthright and his blessing (Genesis 25:29–34, 27:1–39)? What about David, who, after making the mistake of taking refuge with the Philistines (1 Samuel 21:10–22:5), did so again, and was ready to go to war alongside them against the Israelites (1 Samuel 27, 29, 30)?

On and on we could go. The only Bible character who had no regrets is Jesus. The rest of them had plenty. And we have ours as well. And just like these people of long ago, we need God's help to get over our regrets.

We sometimes may feel forgiven but still regret the consequences of our actions. God's forgiveness cannot change the facts of history. We may have to face the reality of some painful outcomes. David could not by his contrition undo the death of Uriah, nor could he bring back to life his dead child. And there were other results as well: his children imitated his duplicity and his murderous ways. They rebelled against David and against God. There are consequences to sin, even when we repent with the heart of David.

We can trust God, though, to extend grace even when
there are dire consequences. God does not abandon us. He
will discipline us, to be sure. But he forgives. And he will do
more than forgive.

First, he will bring good out of the evil we have done.
Consider Romans 8:28:

> And we know that in all things God works for the good
> of those who love him, who have been called accord-
> ing to his purpose.

This passage does not limit God's working to only the
good things in life. God can take the work of Satan and turn
it against him and bring good out of it. Consider the wrong
done to Joseph by his brothers. Their motive and method
were evil, and they succeeded in their plan. But God was not
thwarted by their sin. He took their evil actions and used
them to bless them, their children, their wives, their father
and their future offspring. Joseph recognized this when he
said, "You intended to harm me, but God intended it for good
to accomplish what is now being done, the saving of many
lives" (Genesis 50:20).

God can use our mistakes to teach and encourage us. The
whole story of Joseph is a great encouragement to those of us
who have experienced wrong treatment at the hands of others.
How many times have we been encouraged by this tragic and
yet wonderful story? How many times have we turned to it
when we felt mistreated, abandoned and deserted? God has,
in his grace, a marvelous capacity to turn the tables.

Second, God can use us in great ways after big mistakes.
I will go so far as to say he can and will use us in even greater
ways than before. I love this passage in Isaiah, written to the
rebellious, but now forgiven children of Israel. It is a long passage, but one I hope you will read attentively:

"But you, O Israel, my servant,
    Jacob, whom I have chosen,
    you descendants of Abraham my friend,
I took you from the ends of the earth,
    from its farthest corners I called you.
I said, 'You are my servant';
    I have chosen you and have not rejected you.
So do not fear, for I am with you;
    do not be dismayed, for I am your God.
I will strengthen you and help you;
    I will uphold you with my righteous right hand.

"All who rage against you
    will surely be ashamed and disgraced;
those who oppose you
    will be as nothing and perish.
Though you search for your enemies,
    you will not find them.
Those who wage war against you
    will be as nothing at all.
For I am the LORD, your God,
    who takes hold of your right hand
and says to you, Do not fear;
    I will help you.
Do not be afraid, O worm Jacob,
    O little Israel,
for I myself will help you," declares the LORD,
    your Redeemer, the Holy One of Israel.

"See, I will make you into a threshing sledge,
    new and sharp, with many teeth.
You will thresh the mountains and crush them,
    and reduce the hills to chaff.
You will winnow them, the wind will pick them up,
    and a gale will blow them away.
But you will rejoice in the LORD
    and glory in the Holy One of Israel."
(Isaiah 41:8–16)

God promises that even after their terrible failure, he will use them again. He is saying that his grace is not limited by consequences. He is saying that in his sovereign love he can overcome human sin and mistakes. He is saying, "I will use you again. You can be my instrument again. I will use you in more powerful ways than before."

Now this is grace in action. This is grace at its most glorious. We do not have to feel that if we have made some big mistake, even one with serious consequences, that God is done with us, that though we may be forgiven we are now discarded to the junk pile. No! God can use us again and in even more powerful ways than before. Think about Moses, who was used to lead the people out of bondage after he committed murder. Think about Peter. Think about a host of other flawed, but forgiven, characters in the Bible.

Think about God's grace. We don't deserve it. We never did before we made our big mistakes. You will find if you have walked with the Lord for very long, that most of your mistakes have been made as a Christian, rather than before you were a Christian. It just works that way. God is good, and his grace is amazing. He can take regret, turn it around, and make us better people when it is all over.

So in reflecting upon the regrets in your life, realize that through them all, God's grace is still triumphant. His grace is not exhausted because of a bad decision you made. There may be consequences from that decision, but God is not finished working through your life.

May these inspired prayers of the Psalmist comfort us, and may they be our prayers as well:

> But as for me, I will always have hope;
>   I will praise you more and more.
> My mouth will tell of your righteousness,
>   of your salvation all day long,
>   though I know not its measure.

I will come and proclaim your mighty acts, O
      Sovereign LORD;
  I will proclaim your righteousness, yours alone.
Since my youth, O God, you have taught me,
    and to this day I declare your marvelous deeds.
Even when I am old and gray,
    do not forsake me, O God,
till I declare your power to the next generation,
    your might to all who are to come.

Your righteousness reaches to the skies, O God,
    you who have done great things.
    Who, O God, is like you?
Though you have made me see troubles, many and
      bitter,
    you will restore my life again;
from the depths of the earth
    you will again bring me up.
You will increase my honor
    and comfort me once again.
    (Psalm 71:14–21)

Restore us again, O God our Savior,
    and put away your displeasure toward us.
Will you be angry with us forever?
    Will you prolong your anger through all genera-
      tions?
Will you not revive us again,
    that your people may rejoice in you?
Show us your unfailing love, O LORD,
    and grant us your salvation. (Psalm 85:4–7)

Chapter 31

Grace and Fear

But I will show you whom you should fear: Fear him who, after the killing of the body, has power to throw you into hell. Yes, I tell you, fear him.

Luke 12:5

"There is no fear of God before their eyes."

Romans 3:18

Since you call on a Father who judges each man's work impartially, live your lives as strangers here in reverent fear.

1 Peter 1:17

Then the church throughout Judea, Galilee and Samaria enjoyed a time of peace. It was strengthened; and encouraged by the Holy Spirit, it grew in numbers, living in the fear of the Lord.

Acts 9:31

We should fear God. The message is clear throughout the Scriptures: God is not to be trifled with, God is holy, and he is our Judge. If we do not stand in awe of God, if we do not hold him in reverence, then we cannot and will not be saved.

Grace does not mean that God is weak. We do no honor to God when we reinvent him into a doddering old man who winks away our sin. If God does not judge sin, forgiveness is meaningless and mercy of no account. God is holy, God is wrathful, and God loathes sin. Grace is amazing because God is all of these things.

Likewise, we do no honor to grace when we minimize the ugliness of sin. The testimony of Old and New Testaments affirm that God is holy, sin is heinous, and the only way to be saved is by a sacrifice of unspeakable cost.

Jesus clearly taught that we should fear God. He, more than any other Biblical figure, spoke of eternity and of the reality of judgment. Jesus spoke in vivid terms of the verities of heaven and of hell. He painted in unforgettable colors the scenes of eternal despair and the fearsome prospect of standing before the judgment bar of God. Consider one example of many that could be cited:

> "Then the King will say to those on his right, 'Come, you who are blessed by my Father; take your inheritance, the kingdom prepared for you since the creation of the world....
>
> "Then he will say to those on his left, 'Depart from me, you who are cursed, into the eternal fire prepared for the devil and his angels. For I was hungry and you gave me nothing to eat, I was thirsty and you gave me nothing to drink, I was a stranger and you did not invite me in, I needed clothes and you did not clothe me, I was sick and in prison and you did not look after me.'
>
> "They also will answer, 'Lord, when did we see you hungry or thirsty or a stranger or needing clothes or sick or in prison, and did not help you?'
>
> "He will reply, 'I tell you the truth, whatever you did not do for one of the least of these, you did not do for me.'
>
> "Then they will go away to eternal punishment, but the righteous to eternal life." (Matthew 25:34, 41–46)

— Why we should fear God — [handwritten margin note]

Jesus speaks to the churches of Asia after he has returned to heaven, many years after they were begun. He comes back and gives instruction, encouragement and affirmation. He also delivers a scathing verdict of judgment.

To the church in Ephesus, which had lost its first love:

> "Yet I hold this against you: You have forsaken your first love. Remember the height from which you have fallen! Repent and do the things you did at first. If you do not repent, I will come to you and remove your lampstand from its place." (Revelation 2:4–5)

To the church in Laodicea, which had become lukewarm:

> "I know your deeds, that you are neither cold nor hot. I wish you were either one or the other! So, because you are lukewarm—neither hot nor cold—I am about to spit you out of my mouth." (Revelation 3:15–16)

Jesus gives these warnings to produce godly fear—not just fear of discipline or of ineffectiveness in ministry. The fear is that of judgment, of a loss of their place in heaven, of the loss of their salvation.

Paradoxically, a reverent fear of God removes unhealthy fear from our lives. Consider these words of Jesus:

> "So do not be afraid of them. There is nothing concealed that will not be disclosed, or hidden that will not be made known. What I tell you in the dark, speak in the daylight; what is whispered in your ear, proclaim from the roofs. Do not be afraid of those who kill the body but cannot kill the soul. Rather, be afraid of the One who can destroy both soul and body in hell. Are not two sparrows sold for a penny? Yet not one of them will fall to the ground apart from the will of your Father. And even the very hairs of your head are all numbered. So don't be afraid; you are worth more than many sparrows." (Matthew 10:26–31)

Fear God, but don't fear man, Jesus said. We need to get our fear in the right place. When we have a reverent attitude toward God, it puts the opinions of others about us in proper perspective. When we stand in awe of God, it cuts other people down to size. Is not one of our greatest fears the loss of human approval? Is that not one of the hang-ups that keeps us unhappy, timid and beaten down? Godly fear even changes the way we look at our ultimate survival. If we know we are going to heaven when we die, then we are ready to really live. We can live confidently, joyfully, happily, knowing that there is nothing another person can do to us to take away our true security in life.

Fear—proper, Biblical fear—does not remove joy from our lives. Not at all. It simply means that our joy stands upon a solid Biblical foundation. It means that our joy is based upon a continued relationship of love with our heavenly Father. Fear does not take away our confidence. As a matter of fact, a healthy fear means that we have a great deal of trust, respect and confidence in God. It means that we trust his word so very much that we accept its truth and live in awe of God.

Paul, the great champion of grace, the man who spoke more powerfully in its establishment and defense than any other Biblical writer, affirms that we should fear God. He warns us, "Work out your salvation with fear and trembling" (Philippians 2:12). He looks out at a lost world and says, "Knowing the fear of the Lord, we persuade men" (2 Corinthians 5:11).

Paul established the essentiality of grace, but it was no contradiction in Paul's mind that Christians must stand in reverent fear of God. The reason is plain: Paul believed, as did the other Biblical writers, that we could lose our salvation. He gave warnings to this effect:

> But now he has reconciled you by Christ's physical
> body through death to present you holy in his sight,
> without blemish and free from accusation—if you con-
> tinue in your faith, established and firm, not moved
> from the hope held out in the gospel. This is the
> gospel that you heard and that has been proclaimed to
> every creature under heaven, and of which I, Paul,
> have become a servant. (Colossians 1:22–23)

There is no contradiction in the surety of being saved by
grace and the possibility of losing our salvation. If we abandon
our trust in God, if we turn away from his grace, if we become
self-willed and disobedient, God will recognize the choice we
have made. It is not that God is eager for us to be lost or that
he delights in it. It means that God has established the principle of recognizing our will, of the right of our decision. The
greatest commandment is to love God. This is a decision we
made when we became Christians. If we choose to "unmake"
that decision, we forfeit our place in heaven.

Grace is freely given, but it can be walked away from. Grace
saves us, but we must remain faithful. Grace is assuredly ours,
but not if we deliberately turn away from God. The writer of
Hebrews warns:

> We must pay more careful attention, therefore, to
> what we have heard, so that we do not drift away. For
> if the message spoken by angels was binding, and
> every violation and disobedience received its just pun-
> ishment, how shall we escape if we ignore such a
> great salvation? This salvation, which was first
> announced by the Lord, was confirmed to us by those
> who heard him. (Hebrews 2:1–3)

> If we deliberately keep on sinning after we have
> received the knowledge of the truth, no sacrifice for
> sins is left, but only a fearful expectation of judgment
> and of raging fire that will consume the enemies of

God. Anyone who rejected the law of Moses died without mercy on the testimony of two or three witnesses.
How much more severely do you think a man deserves
to be punished who has trampled the Son of God
under foot, who has treated as an unholy thing the
blood of the covenant that sanctified him, and who
has insulted the Spirit of grace? For we know him who
said, "It is mine to avenge; I will repay," and again,
"The Lord will judge his people." It is a dreadful thing
to fall into the hands of the living God. (Hebrews
10:26–31)

The early church saw no contradiction between fear and
grace (Acts 5:1–11, 9:31). They believed in grace; they lived
in fear. Were they a miserable, guilt-ridden, joyless lot? Far
from it. They feared God and were deeply happy. Theirs was
not the happiness of the ungrateful or the oblivious. Theirs
was not the glee of the casually committed. Theirs was the
joy of those who stood in awe of a mighty God, a God who was
both Father and Judge. They simply had no theological hang-
ups about God's judgment.

Fear is not antithetical to grace. If we are to have a balanced view of God and of the Christian life, we must become
comfortable with the harmonious relationship between godly
fear and godly confidence. It will take maturity and understanding to deal with paradoxical, seemingly contradictory
Biblical teachings. The Scriptures hold some teachings in
tension, and so must we.

Fear is essential. It shows reverence for God. It gives
proper honor to the high cost of grace. It keeps us humble and
dependent upon grace. It keeps us in right relationship to a
holy God. Let us be reverent and fearful, even as we confidently trust in God's unfailing grace.

Chapter 32

Grace and Security

Therefore, there is now no condemnation for those
who are in Christ Jesus....

Romans 8:1

Can we be absolutely, positively confident we are going to
heaven? Can we rest in the security of knowing our souls are
saved and we will be with the Lord forever?

The Bible answers these questions with a resounding,
thunderous, glorious YES!

In the previous chapter we considered the relationship of
grace and fear. We discussed the sobering prospect of losing
our relationship with God and our place in heaven. The good
news is that while the Bible does teach the possibility of losing our salvation, it does not teach the *probability* of it.

For Guilty Souls, the specter of standing before Jesus
after living a life dedicated to serving him and hearing him
say, "I never knew you. Away from me you evildoer," is a very
real one. We wonder if we will end up in the surprised,
despairing multitude who thought they were saved, but
ended up lost. Somehow we feel that maybe we could have
sinned one too many times and that we just might not make
it after all. We think if we died at the wrong moment, after

having an evil thought or a spiritually dull day, that we might not—probably would not—make it to heaven.

What if we missed a morning devotional time or those times had been a bit flat for a while? What if we had selfishly neglected to share our faith or had failed to give money to a homeless person we passed by on the street? What if we had some anger in our heart or a twinge of jealousy lurking in our soul? What if we had some doubt or question in our mind about the Bible? What if on some point of doctrine we were a little off? What if we had not sufficiently sorrowed over or repented of a sin we had committed? What if we were blind to a wrong in our life or there was something which we had not taken as seriously as we should have?

Now that I think about it, I'm getting a little shook up myself.

Thankfully, we can be sure of our salvation for many wonderful reasons. Let me mention a few.

First is simply the *nature of God*. When the Scriptures say that God is faithful (2 Corinthians 1:18–22) and that he does not change like shifting shadows (James 1:17), they are affirming something about God himself. God is not unstable. He is not moody. He is not given to unpredictable or inconsistent behavior. Is not our insecurity often based upon a faulty view of God?

Second, we can be confident because of our *position in Christ.* When we were baptized, we were placed "into Christ" (Romans 6:1–3). Therefore, we are in a solid, stable position. When God looks at us, he does not see us alone, but he sees us as being in Christ. When God looks at us, he sees us as having the goodness and righteousness of Jesus himself. He looks at us through a filter—the righteousness of Jesus—that removes from his sight all of our sin. So great is our position in Christ that the Bible says we have already (in a spiritual sense) been raised with Christ and are seated with him in the heavenly realms (Ephesians 2:6). When we sin, we are not suddenly removed from our position in Christ. We remain there, solidly in union with Christ, and our sin is not counted against us.

Third, we can know we are saved because of the *continually cleansing blood of Christ*. John says, "But if we walk in the light, as he is in the light, we have fellowship with one another, and the blood of Jesus, his Son, purifies us from all sin" (1 John 1:7). The sense of the original language is that the action of the verb "purifies" is continuous, so as to mean "continues to purify us." The blood of Jesus does not just cleanse us once or occasionally. It does its work all day long, all night long, every day of our life for our whole life long!

Fourth, we can be sure because *we have been given the Holy Spirit as a guarantee* of our salvation:

> And you also were included in Christ when you heard the word of truth, the gospel of your salvation. Having believed, you were marked in him with a seal, the promised Holy Spirit, who is a deposit guaranteeing our inheritance until the redemption of those who are God's possession—to the praise of his glory. (Ephesians 1:13–14)

> Now it is God who makes both us and you stand firm in Christ. He anointed us, set his seal of ownership on us, and put his Spirit in our hearts as a deposit, guaranteeing what is to come. (2 Corinthians 1:21–22)

God has given us a great down payment, a security deposit, if you will. He wants us to know that he is serious about getting us all the way home to heaven and that he intends to completely finish the job. He is so determined to make us be and feel secure that he gives his own Spirit to reside in our bodies as an assurance.

And, last, we can be sure of our salvation *because Jesus intercedes in heaven for us*: "Therefore he is able to save completely those who come to God through him, because he always lives to intercede for them" (Hebrews 7:25). At this moment, Jesus is at the right hand of God pleading our case and serving as our mediator. God, the Judge, is already on our side (Romans 8: 31), and Jesus is our advocate. What more could we ask?

Do you still need more convincing? The book of Romans contains the most thorough exposition of grace in the Bible. For seven chapters Paul builds his case. Finally, in the latter half of chapter eight, he breaks into almost rhapsodic celebration of the goodness of grace. It is fitting to bring our thoughts in this chapter to a conclusion by considering what the commentator John Stott calls the five unanswerable questions of chapter 8 of Romans. May they point the way to confidence in our salvation:

> If God is for us, who can be against us? (Romans 8:31)
>
> He who did not spare his own Son, but gave him up for us all—how will he not also, along with him, graciously give us all things? (Romans 8:32)
>
> Who will bring any charge against those whom God has chosen? (Romans 8:33)
>
> Who is he that condemns? (Romans 8:34)
>
> Who shall separate us from the love of Christ? (Romans 8:35)

My dear Guilty Souls, can we, will we not believe that we can close our eyes tonight and sleep in peace, knowing that if we die before we wake, the Lord our soul is sure to take? Can we not live every day in the quiet confidence that we are fully, assuredly saved by the glorious grace of God? Is that not what our Father wants us to know, believe and claim? Isn't it about time we did?

Chapter 33

Grace and Human Approval

Am I now trying to win the approval of men, or of God? Or am I trying to please men? If I were still trying to please men, I would not be a servant of Christ.
Galatians 1:10

This morning I got news that someone is unhappy with me. Not so much me, personally, but with some decisions I had a part in making. Furthermore, there were "other people who felt the same way." You would think that such a circumstance would be but a blip on the screen for a veteran church leader who is no stranger to criticism and disapproval. Not so! I found myself with a quickened pulse and with a cloud of dismay floating above my head. And, of course, I then felt guilty and discouraged that I had these feelings at all and that I was not more mature and faithful in overcoming them.

Human approval is a powerful thing. We are surrounded by people, and they have opinions. They have opinions about everything, and they will have opinions about us. What we do, what we think, what we believe, who we marry, where we work, what we wear, just about everything in our lives.

Guilty Souls are far more affected by human approval than others are. With their lack of confidence and low opinion of themselves, Guilty Souls will naturally be more susceptible to the currents of approval or disapproval. When Guilty Souls lose the blessing of others in reality or imagination, it can send them into a tailspin of anxiety and depression.

The Scriptures certainly teach that we need other people and that we ought to listen to them. Consider these verses:

> The way of a fool seems right to him,
>   but a wise man listens to advice.
> (Proverbs 12:15)

✱ advice

> Pride only breeds quarrels,
>   but wisdom is found in those who take advice.
> (Proverbs 13:10)

✱ Listen

> Listen to advice and accept instruction,
>   and in the end you will be wise.
> (Proverbs 19:20)

It is good to listen to others, and to draw upon their wisdom and experience. And the more godly and exemplary someone's life, the more we should seek and consider their advice.

But we can't please everybody. As Christians we go against the grain of our society. We will be persecuted for our faith. And even with our closest and most spiritual advisors, there will be differences of opinion and disagreement. How do you handle that when it comes? How do you feel when you do not have the approval of someone you care about, someone who loves you and whom you respect?

The Guilty Soul is often cast into despair and guilt when this happens, and things can go downhill from there. When there is conflict, strain or distance in a relationship, the outcome

in the life of a Guilty Soul can be devastating. We Guilty Souls
can so doubt ourselves that we make decisions geared to gain
human approval rather than please God—and later live to regret
them. We can end up blaming ourselves for our cowardly mistake. Or we blame the other person for being manipulative,
controlling and dominating. Obviously, all of that is bad for us
and for our relationships. It is hard to be authentically close to
someone else when you are so afraid of the loss of their approval
that you will not disagree with them.

So, how can grace help?

First, grace assures us that we are accepted by God as we
are. This helps keep human approval in its proper place. Our
relationship with God is not based upon our perfection. How
much more, then, should our relationships with our less-than-
perfect friends not be based on our perfection?

Second, grace means that what others think is not the ultimate judgment upon our lives. God is the most important
Judge, the only one who really counts, and we are therefore
free from being dependent upon human approval for our
sense of happiness or self-worth. What great freedom this
brings! Popularity and approval are such fickle gods anyway.
Can you ever have the approval of *everyone*? Can you please all
of your friends? Can you even get complete approval from all
of your most respected, spiritual advisors? Life is too complicated, and there are too many gray areas for everyone to agree
with you and approve of you. It simply throws you into a pit
of misery to try to win, and keep, the approval of everyone.

How about the disagreement between Paul and Barnabas
recorded in Acts 15? They strongly differed on a matter of
judgment concerning their young helper, John Mark. He had
deserted them in the midst of one of their campaigns, and

Paul felt he should not rejoin them on the next journey.

Barnabas, however, felt that Mark was ready for the challenge and the opportunity would rebuild his confidence. The two leaders could not come to agreement, and they parted company. Interestingly the Scriptures are silent on who was right and who was wrong! Perhaps there was a grain of truth in both positions, and the best thing was for them to split up and let Barnabas take the young man under his wing and nurture him into full maturity. Paul went on to serve God in mighty ways, and John Mark went on to write the Gospel bearing his name.

Years later, Paul asks Timothy to bring John Mark to him in his Roman cell because "he is helpful to me in my ministry" (2 Timothy 4:11). It all got worked out in time, it seems. Some issues are not black and white, and the Guilty Soul must learn this and allow God to work them out in his own time, in his own way.

We should learn to respect and listen to those who love us and who have a proven spiritual track record. But we must never ultimately base our feelings of peace and confidence in having human approval. This will enable us to build stronger friendships, ones not based on servility or flattery—ones in which we are humble enough to listen and change if need be, but in which we are also strong enough to disagree and yet remain friends.

Grace is amazing. It shows our need for God and for others. Yet it shows us that as much as we need others, we ultimately need God more. We will make many mistakes in dealing with one another. We will approve and disapprove of others imperfectly. Others will make the same mistakes with us. In the midst of this we must not forsake our need for others, and yet we must remember that even our dearest friends are fallible and human. We need their encouragement. We need their love. But, more than anything, we all need grace from God.

Chapter 34

Grace and Criticism

I care very little if I am judged by you or by any human court; indeed, I do not even judge myself. My conscience is clear, but that does not make me innocent. It is the Lord who judges me. Therefore judge nothing before the appointed time; wait till the Lord comes. He will bring to light what is hidden in darkness and will expose the motives of men's hearts. At that time each will receive his praise from God.

1 Corinthians 4:3–5

It is true that some preach Christ out of envy and rivalry, but others out of goodwill. The latter do so in love, knowing that I am put here for the defense of the gospel. The former preach Christ out of selfish ambition, not sincerely, supposing that they can stir up trouble for me while I am in chains. But what does it matter? The important thing is that in every way, whether from false motives or true, Christ is preached. And because of this I rejoice.

Philippians 1:15–18

Who likes to be criticized? Most people dislike it, but Guilty Souls loathe it. Loss of approval produces pain, but criticism brings on agony. Criticism brings out the worst in us: resentment, anger, bitterness, fear, self-doubt, guilt and more. Criticism hits us at our core, in our deepest self. It exposes our pride, uncovers our insecurity, spotlights our doubts.

When we stand up for anything, somebody will criticize. They may say it to our face or gossip behind our back. When it gets back to us, we feel violated, as if a thief has come into our home and stolen something dear and precious. Except in this case, we feel that what has been taken is even more valuable than our material possessions: someone has assaulted our very Self.

Many of us spend our lives trying to avoid criticism, and we sometimes compromise our standards in the effort. And, for the Guilty Soul, knowing this tendency causes extreme discomfort, and giving in to it can result in a fresh descent into the pits of self-condemnation. When we sense ourselves playing up to people, something inside us recoils and withers. We realize that we are not being true to God or to our convictions; then we live in the shadow of self-condemnation, and we lose self-respect.

But there is another possible response: to fight back. We fight back with anger, sarcasm and bitterness. We fight back with gossip, name-calling and labeling. We fight back with revenge fantasies, and we seemingly cannot get our mind on anything else. Our critic may have long ago forgotten the slight, but it is to us as if it happened yesterday. We are the producers and directors of our own movie, and we watch it over and over. It makes us miserable and robs us of the tender heart of Christ, but we can't seem to get ourselves out of its clutches.

How can grace help us?

First, we need to see how graciously Jesus handled criticism. While all of his criticism was undeserved and unfair, some, or much, of ours may not be. But still, we can learn from the Lord's example. We deepen in our love and respect for Jesus when we see how calmly and lovingly he responded to his critics. How great was his compassion and how loving his heart in that he never retaliated! That which angers us tells us a very great deal about ourselves. Jesus was not angered when others attacked or criticized him; he became angry when the weak were abused or God's honor was assaulted. Jesus was so concerned with honoring, pleasing and obeying God that he did not allow what people thought about him to bother him. Isn't it usually true that we get angry or lose confidence because we are too focused on others and ourselves—and not focused enough on God?

Second, we must extend grace to our critic. This is not easy to do. The critic may be misinformed, careless or even malevolent. The example of Jesus again comes to our aid. Our Lord refused to let the attitude of another determine his own. Not that he was naive or oblivious, but he simply had another way he thought and lived. He lived by the standard of love and graciously gave to the undeserving.

So must we extend grace. We must be as kind to others as Jesus has been to us. Many critical people are living out a life that is the only one they know. Their sarcasm and put-downs are ways of trying to elevate themselves. They know only the tactic of payback and getting ahead at any cost. How is their pattern to change? It will not change by us retaliating or exacting revenge. God's wisdom says that we help change others by grace, the same way he changed us. We may need to absorb some abuse, even while standing up against it, but we must not respond in kind.

The worst thing we can do is to forget grace when we are criticized. If we forget that we were saved by the cross, by the blood of Christ shed for us, then there is no way we can extend grace to others. We are then headed to anger, bitterness or fear.

Third, <u>we must learn from our critic and from the criticism</u>. Listen carefully to the critic. Is there truth in what he says? Learn from it. It is <u>the truth that sets us free</u>. Was there something selfish or sinful in your reaction when you were criticized? Let this humble you and make you more dependent on grace. Is there nothing you can conscientiously or reasonably do to resolve the situation or change your critic's mind? Then turn the other cheek, and let God judge. Vengeance is his property, not ours.

Like Jesus we are to entrust our way to the Lord (<u>1 Peter 2:23</u>). We are to take the situation to God and leave it with him to work out. When we are dealing with difficult people and situations, we must remember this verse: "<u>If it is possible, as far as it depends on you, live at peace with everyone</u>" (<u>Romans 12:1</u>). Sometimes it is appropriate to defend ourselves and set the record straight. At other times it may be best to be silent and let God work it out in his way, over time. A humble heart is willing to do either.

Guilty Souls are often extremists in dealing with criticism. Because it stings us so much, we may utterly reject the criticism and the critic. When we do this, we can lose a relationship. We also lose the possible benefits of the criticism, and we may lose our righteous attitude. The other extreme is to wither before the criticism and, out of guilt and insecurity, assume it is totally justified and correct. This response makes us victims of whoever may take us to task. It does not lead to authentic growth, and it does not build true relationships with others. It is far better to handle criticism from the posture of confidence in God and security in his grace. If our security is not based on human approval or on our having to be perfect, we will not be so threatened and reactionary when we are criticized. We can instead objectively evaluate it and respond in a godly manner.

In my walk as a Christian, nothing has tested or humbled me more than being unfairly criticized. It has tested my heart and exposed my weaknesses more than any other trial. It has caused me to cast myself upon God more than anything else I have known. I wish it were otherwise, but this is the lesson I have had to learn and am still learning.

In my ministry career I have been criticized for being too aloof and too outspoken. I have been criticized for being too easy and too hard. I have been criticized for preaching too much about grace and too much about works. I have been accused of being too intellectual and too ignorant. I have been told I am too solemn and too flippant. I have been accused of being both a tightwad and a wastrel. It has been said I have too many big dreams and not enough vision. Fact is, there are elements of truth in all of those criticisms. If it were not for the grace of God, I could not be a Christian, let alone a minister. I desperately need grace. I need it from God. I need it from my fellow Christians. I need it from my wife and children. And I need to show it to others, even when they do not show it to me.

The great temptations of being criticized are two: bitterness and loss of confidence. Both are cancerous and destructive. They can only be conquered by, and through, grace. When we stay focused on Jesus and his cross and on God and his grace, we can find the strength not only to endure, but triumph over criticism.

Charles Spurgeon wrote a piece in commenting on Psalm

37 that has helped me weather a recent storm of criticism. I share it with you in hopes that it encourages you as it has me.

> In the matter of personal reputation we may especially be content to be quiet, and leave our vindication with the Judge of all the earth. The more we fret in this case the worse for us. Our strength is to sit still. The Lord will clear the slandered. If we look to his honour, he will see to ours. It is wonderful how, when faith learns to endure calumny with composure, the filth does not defile her, but falls off like snow-balls from a wall of granite. Even in the worst cases, where a good name is for awhile darkened, Providence will send a clearing like the dawning light, which shall increase until the man once censured shall be universally admired. "And thy judgment as the noonday." No shade of reproach shall remain. The man shall be in his meridian of splendor. The darkness of his sorrow and his ill-repute shall both flee away.

> To hush the spirit, to be silent before the Lord, to wait in holy patience the time for clearing up the difficulties of Providence—that is what every gracious heart should aim at. "Aaron held his peace: 'I opened not my mouth, because thou didst it.'" A silent tongue in many cases not only shows a wise head, but a holy heart. "And wait patiently for him." Time is nothing to him; let it be nothing to thee. God is worth waiting for. "He never is before his time, he never is too late." In a story we wait for the end to clear up the plot; we ought not to prejudge the great drama of life, but stay till the closing scene, and see to what finis the whole arrives. "Fret not thyself because of him who prospereth in his way, because of the man who bringeth wicked devices to pass." There is no good, but much evil, in worrying your heart about the present success of graceless plotters: be not enticed into premature judgments—they dishonor God, they weary

yourself. Determine, let the wicked succeed as they may, that you will treat the matter with indifference, and never allow a question to be raised as to the righteousness and goodness of the Lord. What if wicked devices succeed and your own plans are defeated! There is more of the love of God in your defeats than in the successes of the wicked.[1]

---

[1] Charles Haddon Spurgeon, *The Treasury of David, Volume Two* (Grand Rapids: Baker, 1983), 190. (Reprinted from the original seven-volume edition, printed in London by Passmore and Alabaster, 1882–1887.)

Chapter 35

The Grace to Forgive

The LORD is compassionate and gracious,
    slow to anger, abounding in love.
He will not always accuse,
    nor will he harbor his anger forever;
he does not treat us as our sins deserve
    or repay us according to our iniquities.

Psalm 103:8–10

Bear with each other and forgive whatever grievances you may have against one another. Forgive as the Lord forgave you.

Colossians 3:13

This has not been an easy chapter to write. While writing it I realized I had some forgiving to do. I had to stop, get up and pray about a situation in which I knew I had not forgiven. I saw that I was carrying unresolved anger and hurt feelings. I laid the situation before God and told him I knew I was wrong to have the hard feelings I had. I let God know that I wanted to forgive, that I chose to forgive, and that because of my own sins against God that I had no right to withhold forgiveness from this brother who had hurt me.

I cannot say that at this moment my emotions are in any better shape. But I know that I have admitted my sin of unforgiveness, that I have changed my mind about the situation, and that I have asked God to help me forgive as I should.

If you have a hard time accepting grace for yourself, you may have a hard time extending it to others. We tend to treat others as we think we have been treated. Someone who appreciates being forgiven is much more likely to forgive others. Remaining in a guilty state before God leaves you less likely to forgive others. If you cannot accept God's forgiveness for yourself, why would you give it to someone else?

If the Lord is eager to forgive and quickly forgives, you can do the same with others. If, on the other hand, you think that God harbors grudges, that he is slow to forgive, and that he forgives but always holds it over your head, you will tend to do the same to others. If you are not sure God completely forgives, but reserves some vestige of resentment and disapproval, will you not do the same?

God was willing to forgive you before you understood how much you had hurt him.

Jesus prayed to God to forgive those crucifying him even as they were driving the nails in his hands and feet. He did not seek vengeance, he did not even ask that they understand their wrong. He wanted them to be forgiven.

We are here entering into a rarified spiritual climate. It is not easy to forgive. It is my judgment that forgiveness is the single most difficult spiritual challenge for us. The problem with forgiving is that we must be sinned against before we have to do it. We must suffer injury, be treated unjustly, in order to demonstrate this most difficult spiritual quality. As C. S. Lewis said, "Everyone says forgiveness is a lovely idea until they have something to forgive."[1] We feel justified in wanting revenge or in withholding forgiveness because of the

---

[1] C. S. Lewis, *The Joyful Christian* (New York: Scribner, 1996), 141.

wrong that has been done to us. But we are never more like God, or like Jesus, than when we forgive.

If we wait until someone knows exactly how much they have hurt us and how deep is our pain, we will never be able to extend forgiveness. Not one of us knows the depth of pain that Jesus went through to forgive us. Not one of us knows the depth of hurt God felt when his Son cried out, "My God, my God, why have you forsaken me?" as he bore our guilt. None of us knows the restraint God exercised as he withheld sending the legions of angels to relieve the suffering and loss he and his Son bore that day. We never will.

Should we try to understand? Should we grow in our understanding? Should we repent of hardness of heart towards the sufferings of Jesus? The answer to all of these questions is a resounding "yes," but in spite of our best efforts, we will never know these things as the Father and the Son know them. Since God does not require this understanding from us, how can we require it of someone else?

We must think more about the grace God has extended us than the wrongs others have done to us. Gratitude and humility must overcome judgment and hurt feelings.

This does not mean that we should not let others know when they have hurt us. There is a time for that. But sometimes, even when we have done so, they may not see it at all, or they may not see it as we do. What then? We should extend grace and leave the matter in the hands of God.[1] We cannot seek revenge—vengeance belongs to God. Are we to carry bitterness in our hearts? Bitterness solves nothing, and only creates more misery. It does more harm to us than the other person. As someone has said, "Bitterness is the poison we drink, hoping it kills the other person."

---

[1] Study Psalm 37 for encouragement in this area.

If someone is our enemy and is actively seeking to harm us, we can take measures to protect ourselves. We do not have to remain in a situation that is destructive. But there may come a time when we are being wronged and there is nothing we can do to protect ourselves or change the situation. We must extend grace and trust God to deliver us, in keeping with his will. If God does not deliver us from it, then we must depend on his grace to help us endure it, grow from it, and be used for his purposes in it. In the meantime, we must not allow anger, bitterness and unforgiveness to reign in our thoughts or in our hearts.

I realize that what I am saying is difficult to do. I know it is because I have faced some situations that have tested my heart and faith as never before. I have sometimes thought that I appreciated God's grace and that I could extend it easily to others. But then, the tests have come. At different times in my life, people I trusted have let me down. I felt used. I felt undermined. I felt marginalized. In my view, they were ungrateful. They slandered me. I felt deserted when I desperately needed their friendship, understanding, love and support. For me to say it less bluntly would be false to the truth.

Granting forgiveness does not mean we minimize the truth. It means we face the truth, but that we also face a greater and more profound truth. Whatever someone else has done to me, I have done worse to Jesus. It was my sin that caused him to have to go to the cross. If I can face that truth and deeply believe it, I can find the way to forgiveness. In fact, this is the only way to true forgiveness.

At times I have simply had to imagine myself at the foot of the cross, with the blood of Jesus literally falling upon me, in order to finally forgive. It is that serious, that graphic, that ugly. Only then have I found a way to crucify the feelings of anger, betrayal, disappointment and bitterness. Only then have I healed from the wounds. Only when I remember Jesus can I fight those feelings when they return to tempt me again. Only then can I draw the strength to love again, to trust again, to try to help people again, knowing that I will be hurt again. When I can remember that Jesus died for me when I was helpless, a sinner, an enemy and ungodly, only then do I have the means to neutralize the overwhelming, surging acid of bitterness.

The grace of God softens our hearts. It reasons with our minds. It empowers our will. It heals our emotions. It leaves us not merely forgiving, but triumphant. Not merely free, but empowered—empowered to love again, to live again, to be happy again.

Chapter 36

Free at Last!

Awake, awake, O Zion,
    clothe yourself with strength.
Put on your garments of splendor,
    O Jerusalem, the holy city.
The uncircumcised and defiled
    will not enter you again.
Shake off your dust;
    rise up, sit enthroned, O Jerusalem.
Free yourself from the chains on your neck,
    O captive Daughter of Zion.

Isaiah 52:1–2

It is for freedom that Christ has set us free. Stand firm, then, and do not let yourselves be burdened again by a yoke of slavery.

Galatians 5:1

You are free at last! Jesus has died to free you. You are no longer under condemnation. The price of your sin has been paid, the guilt washed away, and continually washed away, by the blood of Jesus. You have a permanent place in the heart of God and in his family. You have the Holy Spirit as your guide, comforter, advocate and power-source. God is actively working out everything in your life for your good. God listens to your prayers and wisely answers them, knowing what is best

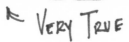

← VERY TRUE

for you. You have the promise of heaven in the next life. What are you waiting for? Walk free! <u>Your chains are broken</u>; <u>live life as a free person</u>!

There are some chains we must decide to remove from our own necks. God has done his part, he has broken them: now we must do ours. Take the chains off. They are rusty, heavy and burdensome. Throw them away, fling them away as far as you can. Get rid of them forever.

It is a tragedy for us to put our chains back on again after God has removed them. He wants you to take them off. Believe him when he says this.

The prodigal son came home, grief-stricken and broken. He volunteered to live in the back, in the servants' quarters: "I have sinned against heaven and against you," he said. "I am no longer worthy to be called your son" (Luke 15:21). He was right, but his father would have nothing of it: "Quick! Bring the best robe and put it on him. Put a ring on his finger and sandals on his feet. Bring the fattened calf and kill it. Let's have a feast and celebrate. For <u>this son of mine was dead and is alive again</u>; <u>he was lost and is found</u>" (Luke 15:22–24).

The Parable of the Lost Son.

This is the heart of God for you. <u>You don't get what you deserve. You get honor and a party.</u> Go to the party! Some of us Guilty Souls have joined with the bitter older brother and have forsaken our own party. The Father has invited us in and we stay outside. The Father has given us a robe, a ring and new sandals; and we have stripped them off, preferring to live in misery and squalor.

I don't know about you, but I'm tired of being outside, not enjoying my own party. I'm going to go in and celebrate. I'm going to take off the chains and put on my garments of splendor. I'm going to take my Father at his word. I'm going to believe he loves me, and loves me a lot. I'm going to believe he delights in me, that I am the apple of his eye. I am going to live like a prince, not like a hireling or a slave. I'm going to let myself go, have a good time, and enjoy life in my Father's house. You know why? Because he wants me to. That is what he has said in his word, and I have nowhere else to go for information. I have had some crazy, wrong ideas in my head, but that is just what they are—crazy and wrong. They are not from God; they are from somewhere else, somebody else.

I'm going to rise up, not stay down. I'm going to hold my head up, not with arrogance, but with confidence. I'm going to sit enthroned, not grovel enslaved. I have been lifted up to sit with Christ in the heavenly realms (Ephesians 2:6), and I might as well enjoy it. I don't deserve it, never can, never will. But it is mine by right of gift—the gift of God. It is the gift of my Father, paid for by my older brother. I know I will never understand it. I can only accept it, enjoy it, celebrate it, smile about it. I can simply live in peace and contentment, knowing this glorious inheritance is mine.

Life will have its disappointments, and they will hurt. I will fail at times. I will sin and disappoint myself and my Father. That does not matter. My Father knew this would happen before he ever called me. With his help, I can overcome these failures and disappointments.

At my best moments, I am so very far from who Jesus was. I can't even get close to Paul. There are some saints I have met that absolutely put me to shame. When I am at my strongest, sin still crouches at my door. I look at all that I could have done or should have done, or all that I have thought, imagined and felt that is so different from what God would have me be, and I realize that I have a long, long way to go.

I always will. I want to remember this and never fall into complacency. But I want to be at peace even when I see the seeming infinity of changes left for me to make. I want to be thankful that I am saved by grace. I want to always remember with gratitude that my sins have been, and are continually being, washed away by the blood of Jesus

Voices will speak to me, saying that this is not so. They will say that I should not take advantage of this, that I should be wary and cautious, that perhaps underneath it all, God is really not so good and caring. That does not matter, and those voices I will dismiss. They are lying voices. They are not from above, but from below. I know at times they will undermine me and drag me down. But I will recover and listen again to my Father's voice. He will win the day. He will get through to me. I will listen as he keeps speaking. And the longer I live, the more I will believe that I am free, and that I am a beloved child, dwelling in peace, joy and love, safe in my Father's house.

> Therefore, since we have been justified through faith, we have peace with God through our Lord Jesus Christ, through whom we have gained access by faith into this grace in which we now stand. And we rejoice in the hope of the glory of God. (Romans 5:1–2)

CPSIA information can be obtained at www.ICGtesting.com
Printed in the USA
BVOW040009100112

280019BV00001B/7/P